HR | Human Resource Management

MANAGING EMPLOYEES FROM RECRUITMENT TO TERMINATION

MADE EASY!

CALIFORNIA CHAMBER of COMMERCE℠

Helping California Business Do Business ®

Published by
California Chamber of Commerce
P.O. Box 1736
Sacramento, CA 95812-1736

ISBN 1-57997-081-8

5 4 3 2 1

The information compiled in this handbook is being provided by the California Chamber of Commerce as a service to the business community. Although every effort has been made to ensure the accuracy and completeness of this information, the California Chamber of Commerce and the contributors and reviewers of this publication cannot be responsible for any errors and omissions, nor any agency's interpretations, applications and changes of regulations described herein.

This publication is designed to provide accurate and authoritative information in a highly summarized manner with regard to the subject matter covered. It is sold with the understanding that the publisher and others associated with this publication are not engaged in rendering legal, technical or other professional service. If legal and other expert assistance is required, the services of competent professionals should be sought.

This publication is available from:

California Chamber of Commerce
P.O. Box 1736
Sacramento, CA 95812-1736
(916) 444-6670
http://www.calchamberstore.com

About the Editor

Paul Schechter is Employment Law Counsel for the Business Services Division of the California Chamber of Commerce. In that position Paul is responsible for the *California Labor Law Digest*, *HRCalifornia*, and the bi-weekly *Labor Law Extra* newsletter, and other reference materials on employment law and human resources practice.

Paul earned B.S. in Economics and Industrial Relations from the Illinois Institute of Technology and his J.D. from Loyola University, Chicago. He was appointed Assistant to the Board Attorney and then Labor Relations Director for the City Colleges of Chicago.

Paul practiced employment and labor relations law on behalf of management as a partner in private law practice. He has been a human resources executive for the Atlantic Richfield Company, and the JC Penney Company in the Midwestern United States, and Human Resources and Labor Relations Director for HCA Healthcare Corporation and Sutter Health in California. He also owned and operated two California retail businesses.

With this background of more than 25 years in the field, Paul draws upon the legal knowledge gained as an employment attorney representing large and small business as well as practical experience as a business owner and human resources executive.

Paul has written articles on employment law subjects for several publications and spoken before local and statewide employer groups on both the legal and practical aspects of human resources management.

Table of Contents

Helping California Business Do Business®

What's New for 2004?

The 2004 *Managing Employees from Recruitment to Termination* is a substantial revision of the California Chamber's previously popular publication, *California Hiring & Termination*. This preface highlights changes and additions in this edition.

Managing Employees from Recruitment to Termination guides you through employment issues, from your initial effort to recruit employees to navigating the employee termination process. We have added new material, such as managing plant closings and layoffs and significantly expanded several topics, including interviewing techniques, performance evaluations and job descriptions.

New Laws

This section offers a brief description, in chapter order, of new laws and court decisions discussed for the first time in this book.

Recruiting Qualified Applicants

- California now outlaws discrimination based on an applicant's gender or gender identity. See "Avoiding Discrimination in Job Advertisements" in Chapter 3, page 54.

- The Equal Employment Opportunity Commission (EEOC) has implemented a new electronic filing process for its *form EEO-1*. See "The Law Explained" in Chapter 3, page 56.

Interviewing and Selecting Qualified Employees

- A recent 9th Circuit Court decision narrows last year's U.S. Supreme Court ruling denying employment to an applicant because the job would present a direct threat to the applicant's health or safety. See "Disability Discrimination" in Chapter 4, page 66.

- A discussion of the recent California court decision regarding an employer's successful defense against a female employee's claim of unequal pay for equal work is included. See "Equal Pay Laws" in Chapter 4, page 81.

- Under a new exemption rule, California permits deductions from an exempt employee's salary for absences due to jury duty, witness duty or military service provided the employee has provided no work during the workweek. See "Forbidden Salary Deductions" in Chapter 4, page 90.

Getting New Employees Started Right

A recent decision from the 9th Circuit Court states that it is *not* unlawful discrimination to terminate an employee who refuses to sign an agreement to arbitrate Title VII claims. See "The Law Explained" in Chapter 5, page 129.

Disciplining and Terminating Employees

- New California law expands protections for current and former employees who report violations of laws or regulations to government agencies. See "Whistleblower Protection" in Chapter 8, page 161.

- A California Court recently decided that employers violate employees' constitutional privacy rights by engaging in disciplinary action in front of other employees. See "Documenting Disciplinary Actions" in Chapter 8, page 166.

- A new National Labor Relations Board ruling states that non-union employees may request but do not have the right to representation during investigatory interviews. See "Investigating Misconduct" in Chapter 8, page 164.

New to this Book

This section provides an overview of topics that are either new to this book or have been substantially revised.

Understanding Your Workforce

This new chapter provides an in–depth discussion of the types of workers who make up the modern workforce, including full- and part-time regular employees, minors, telecommuters, independent contractors, home workers, foreign workers, leased employees and independent contractors. See Chapter 2, "Understanding Your Workforce,"starting on page 13.

Recruiting Qualified Applicants

- A new section about job descriptions, including sample forms and templates, will assist you in developing job descriptions. See "Why You Need Job Descriptions and What They Contain" in Chapter 3, page 45.

- A discussion about job specifications, including sample forms and templates, will assist you in preparing job specifications. See "Preparing the Job Specification" in Chapter 3, page 50.

- Sources you can use to find people qualified to fill open positions are discussed in a new section. See "Identifying Sources for Applicants" in Chapter 3, page 51.

Interviewing and Selecting Qualified Employees

- Find expanded guidance on screening applications and interviewing applicants. See "What You Should Do" in Chapter 4, page 69.

- An expanded discussion regarding testing applicants and conducting background is included. See "Learning About Your Applicants" in Chapter 4, page 72.

- There is a in–depth discussion of issues to consider when determining starting pay. See "Determining Starting Pay" in Chapter 4, page 81.

Evaluating Employee Performance

This chapter contains expanded information to guide you through the process of preparing for and delivering employee performance evaluations. See Chapter 6, "Evaluating Employee Performance," starting on page 141.

Conducting Reorganizations and Workforce Reductions

This new chapter discusses plant closings and layoffs, including the federal and state laws mandating notice to government, employees and employee representatives. See Chapter 7, "Conducting Reorganizations and Workforce Reductions,"starting on page 149.

Disciplining and Terminating Employees

This chapter provides you with guidance about creating and administering a multi–step (progressive) discipline program. See "Multi–Step (Progressive) Discipline" in Chapter 8, page 163.

Chapter 1

Getting Started

This book is a practical, hands–on and easy–to–use guide to making decisions about the selection, evaluation, discipline and termination of your workforce. Much of the information on termination applies to involuntary and voluntary terminations.

The CD that comes with this product contains all the legally required employment forms for both recruitment and termination. It also contains forms that are recommended to help your company avoid unnecessary litigation and make your job easier. Each form is clearly marked to identify whether it is required or recommended. The CD that comes with this product also contains forms necessary to evaluate the performance of your workforce in support of its retention, training or termination.

This book gives a clear and concise explanation of why, when and how to use each form and what to do with it once you have completed it. Most forms have corresponding filled in samples so you can see how the forms are used. Checklists are provided throughout so you can tell, at a glance, if you have complied with the law, as well as with your own personnel policies. Use the checklists as is or modify them to suit your needs.

Each chapter in this book takes you through a different stage in the employment relationship and contains material designed to alert you to basic legal issues that you should keep in mind at each stage. Particular care has been taken to make this book concise and straightforward, to avoid "legalese," and to answer the questions most often asked by employers. At times you may have questions about particular personnel issues that go beyond the scope of this book. For more information, refer to these California Chamber's related products:

- *2004 California Labor Law Digest*;

- *California Human Resource Essentials*;

- *Employee Handbook: How to Write One for Your Company*; and

- *Managing to Avoid Sexual Harassment Liability*.

Additionally, the California Chamber offers services and support via our **HR California** website at ***http://www.hrcalifornia.com***.

Take some time now to familiarize yourself with the format of this book and its checklists and forms. You don't have to wait until the next time you hire an employee to make use of this book. Starting today, you can:

- Use the attendance tracker for current employees (see "Attendance Control" in Chapter 8, page 168);

- Pass out the brochures and information required by law that you have not previously distributed (see "What Forms and Checklists Do I Use to...?" at the end of each chapter);

- Collect emergency information about your employees (see "Emergency Contact Information" in Chapter 5, page 125);

- Review the applicant reference checking forms to protect yourself from a possible "negligent hiring" lawsuit (see "Reference Checks" in Chapter 4, page 76); and

- Use the disciplinary and termination forms when necessary (see Chapter 8, "Disciplining and Terminating Employees").

As referring to this book becomes an everyday experience, you'll find that the sections of the book come together to form a complete system for managing your employees. Keep in mind that the benefits of using this book are only as good as the effort of the people using it. Make sure that managers and supervisors using the forms contained here are properly trained in their use. Likewise, make sure that the forms are being used in a uniform manner throughout your workplace.

Of course we can't guarantee that using this book will make every member of your workforce a model employee. However, we can assure you that using this book will help you make recruitment and termination decisions that comply with the law and make costly litigation far less likely.

Required Posters

You must display required posters at each work site and place them in an area frequented by all employees. Make sure that you display the most current versions of each poster because state and federal agencies periodically make changes. To find out more about poster updates after the date of this printing, visit the California Chamber store at *http://www.hrcalifornia.com/poster*.

Use the following table to identify the posters that you are required to display. You can also view a sample *Required Posters for the Workplace* chart on the CD that comes with this product. The poster titles in the table are arranged in the order that they appear in the California Chamber's *Employer Poster* product, which is available in our online store at *http://www.calchamberstore.com*.

Table 1. Required Posters

Title	Who must post?	Source	Version/Date
Emergency Phone Numbers	All employers	Dept of Industrial Relations/Division of Occupational Safety & Health	S–500 March 1990
Pay Day Notice	All employers	Dept of Industrial Relations	No version number No date
Safety and Health Protection on the Job	All employers	Dept of Industrial Relations/Division of Occupational Safety & Health	No version number August 2003
Notice to Employees – Injuries Caused by Work	All employers	Division of Workers' Compensation	DWC Form 7 (07/04)
Discrimination or Harassment in Employment is Prohibited by Law	All employers	Dept of Fair Employment and Housing	DFEH 162 (01/04)
California Minimum Wage	All employers	Industrial Welfare Commission	MW-2002
Federal Minimum Wage	All employers	Federal Dept of Labor	WH Pub. 1088 Revised Oct 1996
Both the state and federal minimum wage posters must be posted, even though California's minimum wage is currently higher than the federal minimum wage.			
Pregnancy Disability Leave	Employers of 5-49 employees and all public agencies	Dept of Fair Employment and Housing	DFEH 100–21 (01/00)
Your Rights Under the Federal Family and Medical Leave Act of 1993	Employers of 50 or more employees and all public agencies	Federal Dept of Labor	WH Pub. 1420 Revised Aug 2001
Equal Employment Opportunity in the Law	All employers	Equal Employment Opportunity Commission	EEOC–P/E–1 Revised 9/02
Time Off for Voting	All employers. Must be posted for 10 days preceding statewide election.	California Secretary of State	No version number No date

Table 1. Required Posters

Title	Who must post?	Source	Version/Date
Notice Employee Polygraph Protection Act	All employers	Federal Dept of Labor	WH Pub. 1462 September 1988
Notice to Employees – Unemployment Insurance, State Disability Insurance and Paid Family Leave	Most employers	Employment Development Department (EDD)	DE 1857A Rev. 35 (10–03)
Protection for Employee Whistleblowers	All employers	Office of the Attorney General	No version number (1/1/04)
Log and Summary of Occupational Injuries and Illnesses (Log 300)	High hazard employers of 10 or more employees, for the month of February 2003.	Dept of Industrial Relations/Division of Occupational Safety and Health	No version number No date
Wage Order (17)	All employers must post the industry – specific Wage Order for their business	• Dept of Industrial Relations • California Chamber's website, **HR California**, at **http://www.hrcalifornia.com/wageorders**	There are 17 Wage Orders, with various version dates. For more information, visit the **HR California** website at **http://www.hrcalifornia.com/wageorders**

Other Required Postings

Depending on your industry, you may also be required to post the following:

- IWC Wage Orders – All employers must post the industry–specific Wage Order that is appropriate to their business.

- Log 300 – Not every employer must comply with Cal/OSHA's Log 300 record keeping requirement. To see if you are required to complete the forms, visit **www.hrcalifornia.com/log300** and click the free "Log 300 Exempt Wizard."

Forms

The forms included on the CD that comes with this product were developed by the California Chamber or collected from government agencies. Completed sample forms are included to demonstrate how each one should be filled out. For your convenience, we've clearly indicated whether each form is required by government mandate or recommended for use as a good business practice. With the exception of the forms provided by the government, which are public domain, all other forms are copyrighted by the California Chamber. Purchasers of this book are granted limited license to reproduce blank forms for the sole purpose of use by the purchaser's organization.

Reproduction of these forms for commercial purposes is strictly prohibited.

Records Retention

At this point, questions, such as "What do I do with all of these forms? How long do I keep them?" and "Who may have access to them?" may arise. The following section is a brief overview of:

- How long you must keep each type of record;

- Special rules pertaining to employee privacy, which mandate that certain records may not be kept in an employee's personnel file;

- Which records that various state and federal laws require that you keep;

- Other records that you must/should keep out of personnel files; and

- Laws pertaining to employee access to their personnel files.

How Long to Retain Records

There are at least seven laws, both state and federal, mandating different lengths of time various employment records must be kept.

For the sake of practicality, many employers simply keep the bulk of a former employee's personnel file and other records for the duration of employment plus four years. This practice covers nearly every legal requirement, with the exception of three types of records that must be removed from a file and retained for a longer duration, before the file is disposed of. The three exceptions are:

- Pension and welfare plan information (retain six years);

- First–aid records of job injuries causing loss of work time (retain five years); and

- Safety and toxic/chemical exposure records, including Material Safety Data Sheets (retain 30 years).

 For more information, review the sample *Records Retention Requirements* chart on the CD that comes with this product.

Where to Retain Records

Keep employment records in individual personnel files and restrict access to the files. As personnel files may contain sensitive and private information, always keep them in a locked cabinet. Designate a single individual to control access, from whom authorization must be gained before others may view the files.

Although you may keep the majority of the documents you retain for each employee together in a personnel file, there are certain types of documents that must or should be kept separately:

- Medical records;

- Equal Employment Opportunity classification information; and

- Employment Eligibility Verifications (*I-9 Form*)

Medical Records

California law mandates that you establish appropriate procedures to ensure all employee medical records and information remain confidential and are protected from unauthorized use and disclosure. Failing to establish such procedures is a misdemeanor and allows an employee to collect damages and attorney's fees.

One appropriate procedure for ensuring confidentiality is to establish a second file for each employee to retain information protected by privacy laws. This confidential file may contain medical records and any other sensitive information, such as private financial records. Keep it separate from the regular personnel files and grant access only to those with a legitimate need to know the information.

> **Example:** A supervisor who is considering a particular employee for a promotion to a clerical position in another department probably has no need to know information about that employee's pre–employment physical. On the other hand, if the position to which the employee is being promoted requires heavy lifting, records from the pre–employment physical may be necessary to assess the individual's restrictions or necessary accommodations.

The type of records protected under these laws encompasses more than a physician's report or the lab results from a drug test. Medical records may include:

- Family and medical leave request forms, if an employee voluntarily discloses the nature of his or her illness on such a form;

- Return–to–work releases;

- Workers' compensation records;

- Information about accommodated disabilities; and

- Other records that relate in any way to an employee's medical history.

Equal Employment Opportunity Classification Information

Employers of 15 or more employees are required to maintain a record of the sex, race and national origin of applicants and employees apart from personnel files. These records must be maintained to demonstrate, if necessary, that you are attempting to recruit and develop a workforce reflective of the community's ethnic profile. Keep equal employment opportunity (EEO) records in a common file rather than in each employee's personnel file.

Employment Eligibility Verifications (*I-9 Form*)

Keep forms and information verifying the right of your employees to work in this country (*I-9 Form* and photocopies of verification documents, if made) in a common file rather than in each employee's own personnel file. This practice ensures that the information is easily accessible for an audit by immigration or labor officials. For more information, see "Employing Foreign Workers" in Chapter 2, page 33.

Employees' Access to Their Personnel Files

Employees must have access to their own personnel records, both while employed and after termination of the employment relationship, until the applicable statute of limitations runs out on any possible legal claims. Employees also may grant authorization in writing for any other individual to have such access.

State law has now been standardized so that both public and private sector employees have the right to access their personnel files. Every employee has the right to inspect the personnel records that you maintain relating to his/her performance, or to any grievance concerning him/her.

Inspection may be limited to once a year, unless there is reasonable cause to believe the file has been altered in a manner that might adversely affect the employee's interests, promotion, etc., or if the file contains information that may be pertinent to an ongoing investigation that affects the employee. Notes may be taken about the contents of the file.

Employees may view their files at a reasonable time and place by appointment, usually during business hours in the office where personnel files are maintained, unless another time or place is mutually agreed upon. You may require the employee to view a file during his/her free time. You have the right and responsibility to monitor your employee's inspection of his/her personnel file to ensure that nothing is removed, destroyed or altered and to return the file to the proper place when the inspection is completed.

Employees may not inspect certain records, such as records of criminal investigations or letters of reference maintained by you. On the other hand, employees have a right to a copy of any document they have signed related to obtaining or holding employment, subject to a reasonable fee for each copy.

The following list contains examples of the documents that employees are entitled to inspect:

- Application for employment;

- Application for re-employment;

- Payroll authorization form (hiring agreement);

- Change orders in records on compensation, dates of hire, birth and other changes of status;

- Notices of commendation, warning, discipline or termination;

- Notices of layoff, leave of absence and similar matters;

- Notices of wage attachment or garnishment;

- Notices of union requirements, membership, dues checkoff, etc.;

- Education and training notices and records;

- Medical restrictions;

- Test results;

- Performance appraisal or interview evaluation ratings;

- Attendance and absence records;

- Promotion recommendations;

- Production quality and records (individual);

- Records of grievances affecting employment status;

- Investigation of Fair Employment and Housing Commission (FEHC) or Equal Employment Opportunity Commission (EEOC) matters;

- Unfair labor practice matters;

- Medical records affecting employment status; and

- Records comparing the employee with other employees, such as ratings.

Employees' Access to Their Payroll Records

California law requires employers to provide current and former employees access to payroll records within 21 days of receiving a written or oral request. Current or former employees are permitted to inspect or copy their payroll records. Your failure to comply with this law entitles the current or former employee, or the Labor Commissioner, to a penalty payment of $750. An employee may also take legal action to obtain compliance with the request and is entitled to recover costs and reasonable attorney's fees for such action.

You may not be held liable for failing to comply if it is impossible for you to produce the records. That is, if your inability to produce the records is not the result of your unlawful action, such as prematurely destroying payroll records. For more information about record retention requirements, see "Records Retention" on page 5.

What Forms and Checklists Do I Use to Get Started?

The following table describes forms and checklists that cover some of the background requirements of the employment process.

 You can find these forms on the CD that comes with this product.

Table 2. Recommended Forms and Checklists

Form/Checklist Name	What do I use it for?	When do I use it?	Who fills it out?	Where does it go?
Records Retention Requirements	To check how long to keep personnel records	For reference	No filling out needed	NA
Required Posters for the Workplace	To verify you have the most up-to-date employer posters required by California and federal law, as well as the most current Wage Orders.	For reference	No filling out needed	NA

Where Do I Go for More Information?

The California Chamber and the federal and state governments have a variety of resources to help you recruit, manage and terminate employees in compliance with the law.

Table 3. Additional Resources

For information on	Check out these resources
General	From the California Chamber: • The **California Labor Law Digest**, the most comprehensive, California–specific resource to help employers comply with complex federal and state labor laws and regulations; • **www.calchamberstore.com**; and • **www.hrcalifornia.com**.

Table 3. Additional Resources

For information on	Check out these resources
Consumer Reporting Agencies	Federal Trade Commission Consumer Response Center – FCRA Washington, DC 20580 (202) 326–3761 **www.ftc.gov** *Using Consumer Reports: What Employers Need to Know* at **www.ftc.gov/bcp/conline/pubs/buspubs/credempl.pdf**.
• Employment Discrimination • Equal Opportunity • Sexual Harassment	Equal Employment Opportunity Commission (EEOC) 901 Market Street, #500 San Francisco, CA 94103 (415) 356–5100 **www.eeoc.gov** California Department of Fair Employment and Housing (DFEH) **www.dfeh.ca.gov** You may also contact your local office of the DFEH, listed in your local telephone directory under "Fair Employment and Housing" in the State Government section.
Federal Tax and Benefits Regulation	Internal Revenue Service (IRS) Employers or Plan Coordinators, call: (202) 622–6080 **www.irs.ustreas.gov**
Immigration	United States Citizenship and Immigration Services (USCIS) Office of Special Counsel for Immigration Related Unfair Employment Practices P.O. Box 27728 Washington, DC 20038–7728 **www.uscis.gov** The USCIS Office of Special Counsel has established a toll–free Employer Hotline at (800) 255–8155. The hotline provides pre-recorded information about complying with employment–related immigration laws.
• Paid Family Leave • Reporting New Employees • State Disability Insurance • Unemployment Insurance	Employment Development Department (EDD) New Employee Registry P.O. Box 997350, MIC 99 W. Sacramento, CA 95899–7350 (916) 657–0529 Fax: (916) 255–3211 **www.edd.ca.gov**

Table 3. Additional Resources

For information on	Check out these resources
Pension and Other Benefits Plans	US Department of Labor Pension and Welfare Benefits Administration 200 Constitution Avenue, NW Room N5625 Washington, DC 20210 (202) 219–8776 ***www.dol.gov/dol/pwba***
Wage/Hour and Wage Payment Regulation	California Department of Industrial Relations Division of Labor Standards Enforcement P.O. Box 420603 San Francisco, CA 94141–3660 (415) 557–7878 ***www.dir.ca.gov***
Workers' Compensation	• California Workers' Compensation Institute 1111 Broadway, Suite 2350 Oakland, CA 94607 (510) 663–1063 ***www.cwci.org*** • The California Chamber's ***Managing Workers' Comp and Safety in California***. To purchase a copy of the book, call (800) 331–8877, or visit our online store at ***http://www.calchamberstore.com***. • California Department of Industrial Relations (DIR) Division of Workers' Compensation (DWC) Headquarters 455 Golden Gate Avenue, 9th Floor San Francisco, CA 94102-3660 (800) 736-7401 ***http://www.dir.ca.gov/dwc***

Chapter 2

Understanding Your Workforce

The 21st century workforce is composed of people with a variety of relationships with the organization for which they perform services. Your workforce may include:

- Direct or leased employees, who may work on the company's premises, on the premises of customers or in their own homes or workplaces;

- Workers who may be employed on a project, on a temporary or seasonal basis; and

- Independent contractors.

Before beginning the hiring process, you need to understand the different types of employment relationships available to you, so you can select the one that is appropriate for the job to be performed.

Employment At–Will

Although Labor Code 2750 addresses the "contract of employment," most employer/employee relationships in California are "at–will" employment.

 California law defines the **contract of employment** as one by which the employer engages another, who is called the employee, to do something for the benefit of the employer or a third person.[1]

---

1. California Labor Code section 2750

For workers' compensation purposes, **employee** means every person in the service of an employer under any appointment or contract of hire or apprenticeship, express or implied, oral or written, whether lawfully or unlawfully employed.[2] If you hire someone to perform services for which a contractors license is required — or who performs such services for a person required to obtain such a license — a court or law enforcement agency will assume that person is an employee rather than an independent contractor.[3] You will have the burden of proving otherwise.

 Employment at-will has no specified term and may be terminated at the will of either party on notice to the other. This definition is contrasted with employment for a specified term, which is employment for a period greater than one month.[4]

The Law Explained

California's Labor Code specifies that an employment relationship with no specified duration is presumed to be employment at-will. This means, at least in theory, that the employer or employee may terminate the employment relationship at any time, with or without cause. However, a number of court decisions have seriously eroded California's at-will presumption. Even where no written or oral contract has been made specifying the duration of employment, courts have construed various factors, including employment advertisements and applications, to create an "implied" contract. For example, an implied contract for a certain duration might be found if an employment advertisement describes a "secure position" or asks for candidates willing to make a "long-term commitment to the company." You can create a promise to terminate only for "just cause" through a written, oral or implied contract.

 Just cause means a fair and honest cause or reason, acted on in good faith by the employer.[5]

 Avoid advertisements indicating your company is "like one big happy family" or "looking for someone who can grow with the company." Some of the factors that courts consider in determining whether an implied contract of employment exists include: length of employment, promotions or commendations and lack of job performance criticism received by the employee.

---

2. California Labor Code Section 3351
3. California Labor Code Section 2750.5
4. Labor Code Section 2922
5. *R.J. Cardinal v. Ritchie*, 218 Cal. App. 2d 124 (1963)

Two important California Supreme Court decisions have expanded employer rights. In one decision, the Court granted California employers the right to unilaterally terminate or change policies contained in their employee handbooks without concern for violating an implied contract of employment. A second decision provides that, where an employer has an express policy of at–will employment, an employee generally cannot claim there was an "implied" contract to terminate for just cause only. According to the Court, "longevity, raises and promotions are their own rewards for the employee's continuing valued service," but do not, by themselves, guarantee future employment. Where an employer has an expressed at–will policy, an implied contract of employment will now be found only if the employer has created, through words or conduct, a specific understanding that employment will be terminated for good cause only.

What You Should Do

It is important to have an employee handbook with strong statements regarding your right to terminate or change policies and that employment is at–will and can be terminated at any time with or without cause and with or without notice. The rest of the handbook should not contain policies that are contrary to employment at–will. For example, avoid a statement in your progressive discipline policy that promises a certain number of warnings prior to termination, or a policy that requires employees to give two weeks notice prior to resigning.

Managers and supervisors also must understand that they do not have the authority to promise, either in specific or implied terms, job security to applicants or employees. Either may claim a promise of job security if they've been told by a manager: "Do a good job and you'll always have a job." or "Don't worry, we'll always find a place for you."

Employing Minors

You must pay special attention to state and federal laws and regulations when employing minors. These laws specify:

- When minors may be employed;

- How many hours minors may work; and

- What jobs they may not perform.

In California, a **minor** is defined as any person under the age of 18 who is required to attend school and also includes children under the age of six.

To begin with, you must have a work permit on file when employing a minor.

The Law Explained

A work permit sets limits on the maximum number of days and hours of work allowed for the minor and the spread of hours permitted (i.e., the earliest minors may start work and the latest they may end work each day). It also may contain limitations on other aspects of the minor's work. The back of the work permit contains a summary of restricted occupations based on a minor's age and legal restrictions on hours of work.

 A work permit must be issued before the minor begins working. It is a violation of child labor laws to put a minor to work and then begin the process of applying for a work permit. Permits issued in one school year expire five days after a new school year begins. The school year in California begins July 1 and ends June 30.

No work permit is required for a minor who is a high school graduate. However, federal regulations restrict anyone under the age of 18 from working in certain occupations unless the minor has completed a bona fide course of training in that occupation.

No work permit is required for minors delivering newspapers or working occasionally at odd jobs, such as yard work or babysitting in private homes.

High school dropouts are not excused from the work permit requirements. Emancipated minors must have a work permit, but may apply for one without their parent's permission. Work permits are required even during the summer months and school vacations. Minors employed in California who are not state residents, such as children who reside out of state with one parent during the school year and visit the other parent in California during the summer, must have a California work permit. The local school district in which the minor resides while visiting issues the permit. Even parents employing their own children generally must obtain a work permit.

Penalties

Penalties for child labor violations, including failure to obtain a work permit and violation of work hour limitations, run from $500 to $10,000, depending on the number and type of violations. See the sample *Basic Provisions and Regulations - Child Labor Laws* on the CD that comes with this product for a summary of state and federal child labor laws. Use the sample *Checklist for Employing Minors* on the CD that comes with this product, which summarizes legal issues for you to consider when hiring a minor.

Employing Minors in Specified Industries

A minor employed in the entertainment industry must have an *Entertainment Work Permit* issued by the Division of Labor Standards Enforcement (DLSE). You must also have a *Permit to Employ Minors in the Entertainment Industry*, which the DLSE also issues.

Minors ages 14 and 15 may work providing sports–attending services at professional games until 12:30 a.m. during any evening preceding a non–school day and until 10:00 p.m. any evening preceding a school day. When school is in session, 14– and 15–year–olds may work a maximum of 5 hours per day and 18 hours per week as professional baseball "sports attendants." When school is not in session, they may work a maximum of 40 hours per week.

School authorities who issue the minor's work permit must monitor the academic achievement of the minor to ensure that his/her educational progress is being maintained or improved during the period of employment.

Sixteen– and 17–year–olds employed in agricultural packing plants during the peak harvest season may work up to 10 hours on any day that school is not in session. Before you schedule a minor for over eight hours of work in an agricultural packing plant, you must obtain a special permit from the Labor Commissioner. The permit is granted only if it does not materially affect the safety and welfare of minor employees and prevents you undue hardship. The Labor Commissioner may require an inspection of the packing plant prior to granting the permit. A permit may be revoked after reasonable notice is given in writing, or immediately, if any of its terms or conditions are violated. The Labor Commissioner provides an application for such a permit and a copy of the completed application must be posted at the place of employment at the time the application is submitted. Prior to issuing or renewing an exemption, the Labor Commissioner must inspect the agricultural packing plant.

Lake County Agriculture Exemption

Sixteen– and 17–year–olds who work in agricultural packing plants in Lake County, California, are exempted from the normal working hours limitations. These minors, if enrolled in public or private school in Lake County, may work between 48 and 60 hours per week under an exemption issued by the state Labor Commissioner with prior written approval of the Lake County Board of Education. This exemption was set to be repealed on January 1, 2002, but has been extended to January 1, 2005.

As a condition of receiving an exemption or a renewal of an exemption, you must, on or before March 1 of each year, file a written report to the Labor Commissioner containing the following information regarding the prior year's payroll:

- The number of minors employed; and

- A list of the age and hours worked on a weekly basis of each minor employed.

 For more information, review the sample *Entertainment Work Permit* and the procedures for obtaining it on the CD that comes with this product. See also the *Application for Permission to Work in the Entertainment Industry (DLSE-277)* and *Application for Permission to Employ Minors in the Entertainment Industry (DLSE-281).*

When Work Permits Are Not Required

Work permits are not required for:

- Any minor who is a high school graduate or who has been awarded a Certificate of Proficiency;

- Minors who irregularly work at odd jobs, such as yard work and babysitting in private homes, where the minor is not otherwise regularly employed;

- Minors who are at least 14 years of age and are employed to deliver newspapers to consumers;

- Minors who work for a parent or guardian in agriculture, horticulture, viticulture or domestic labor on or in connection with property the parent or guardian owns, operates or controls. However, these minors may not be employed during school hours, even when they are under school age;

- Minors of any age who participate in any horseback riding exhibition, contest or event, whether or not they receive payment for services or prize money;

- Minors who are self-employed; and

- Minors directly employed by state and local agencies, unless expressly included in the state's Labor Code. State and local agencies are, however, covered by the federal FLSA and must meet all of its requirements.

What You Should Do

Two forms are required under the work permit laws. Before employment begins, you or the minor must obtain the necessary forms. Contact the Office of the Superintendent of the school district in which the minor attends school. Use the sample *Checklist for Employing Minors* on the CD that comes with this product to guide you through the process of employing a minor.

First, if you're considering hiring a minor, you and the minor must complete a *Statement of Intent to Employ Minor and Request for Work Permit (Form B1-1). Form B1-1* should be completed by the minor and signed by you and the parent or guardian of the minor. Once *Form B1–1* is filed with the school district, the district completes and issues a *Permit to Employ and Work (Form B1-4)*. The district may issue a work permit, which specifies:

- The maximum number of hours of work per day when school is in session;

- Other limitations; and

- The expiration date of the permit.

The school district keeps the *Form B1–1* on file. You must keep the *Form B1–4* (work permit) on file as long as you employ the minor. You can either keep work permits in each employee's personnel file or in a common binder for easy review of allowable work hours for all minors you employ. These records must be available at all times for inspection by school authorities and officers of the DLSE.

Minors requesting work permits must have the names of your workers' compensation carrier on their *Form B1–1*. If minors enrolled in work experience education programs are to be paid for their work, you must carry workers' compensation insurance for them. In the case of minors who are not paid for their work in work experience education programs, workers' compensation insurance must be carried by the school district.

You may not pay minors who have graduated from high school or have a Certificate of Proficiency less than adult employees in the same establishment for the same quantity and quality of work. However, differences in pay may be based on:

- Seniority;

- Length of service;

- Ability;

- Skills;

- Difference in duties or services performed;

- Difference in the shift or time of day worked, hours of work; or

- Other reasonable differentiation exercised in good faith.

 For more information, review the sample *Statement of Intent to Employ Minor and Request for Work Permit (Form B1-1)* and *Permit to Employ and Work (Form B1-4))* on the CD that comes with this product.

Paying Subminimum Wage

You may, in limited circumstances, pay minors less than the minimum wage. Both state and federal law regulate these subminimum wages. The federal Opportunity Wage now allows employers to pay a subminimum rate to individuals under the age of 20 for the first 90 consecutive days of employment. State law allows you to pay "learners" 85% of the minimum wage rounded to the nearest nickel, but not less than $5.75. Unfortunately, the overlapping of the state and federal standards severely limits the payment of subminimum wages in California. You may pay apprentices at subminimum rates, but only in accordance with federal standards.

Always check with legal counsel before paying subminimum rates.

The California Chamber's *2004 California Labor Law Digest* devotes an entire chapter to the employment of minors. In addition, California's Department of Industrial Relations (DIR) publishes a booklet entitled *Child Labor Laws* available by written request from:

Department of Industrial Relations
Division of Labor Standards Enforcement
P. O. Box 420603
San Francisco, CA 94142–3660
Special Safety Considerations

Young workers statistically account for a disproportionate number of injuries on the job. The California Department of Industrial Relations has valuable information on its website that can alert you to safety concerns and help prevent injuries to young workers. You can find this information at *http://www.dir.ca.gov/YoungWorker/YoungWorkersMain.html*.

Employing Telecommuters

Telecommuting allows an employee to work at home or at another satellite location. It is often a flexible work arrangement connected to a business using phones, faxes or the Internet. Telecommuting is most appropriate for jobs:

- Requiring concentration and independent work;

- Needing little face–to–face communication; and

- Producing a measurable result.

The Law Explained

Telecommuting arrangements generate a number of legal issues. The first relates to federal and state wage and hour laws. With the employee off–site, it becomes difficult to track time worked, overtime liability, compliance with meal and rest periods and work off–the–clock. Regardless of the challenge, you are responsible for insuring compliance with federal and state wage and hour laws.

Second, although the premises and work station are not under your control, you are still responsible for the safety of your employee. In addition, injuries that arise out of and occur in the course of performing the job are compensable under workers' compensation. Under most circumstances, an employee is not covered for an injury while traveling to or from work, but the result may be different when the employee works off–site. An injury occurring while traveling between work and a home office would likely be considered compensable.

Another issue concerns liability for injuries incurred while working at home. Some of the factors that are considered when determining liability include:

- The regularity with which work is performed at home;

- Whether the home office is being used as a convenience for the employee rather than as required by the employer; and

- Whether there is business equipment and a designated workspace in the home.

Also, recognize that the risk of fraudulent workers' compensation claims is increased by telecommuting programs.

Third, issues may arise regarding confidentiality and privacy, including monitoring how the employee is using email and the Internet, accessing company information and protecting company secrets at the employee's home or other remote locations. An employer's right to monitor, intercept/access its employees' electronic communications is regulated by the federal Electronic Communications Privacy Act of 1986 (ECPA), the wiretap sections of the California Penal Code 630–637.9 and other laws. Monitoring is permitted when in the "ordinary course of business" by the provider of communications service or where one of the parties to the communication gives prior consent to the interception. Email messages may not be monitored if the system is provided by an outside entity, without the authorization of either the employee who communicated the message or its intended receiver.

However, a California court has provided some guidance concerning the protection of company information stored on an employee's work–at–home computer. In a wrongful termination case resulting from an employee's alleged intentional and repeated accessing of sexually explicit websites, the Court said that an employer has the right to examine the contents of the hard drive in a work–at–home computer it had provided to an employee — and to introduce it as evidence in a court proceeding. The employee had no "reasonable expectation of privacy" under the California constitution, where the employee had consented in writing to employer's policy statement that it monitored electronic communications conducted on work–at–home and office computers.[6]

A strongly worded and disseminated policy on Internet security and email usage can help you assert necessary control. In addition, advise and train all employees about handling such information, managing/reporting security breaches and using available encryption technology for transmission of critical information.

Finally, telecommuting may be seen as a reasonable accommodation under the Americans with Disabilities Act (ADA) and the California Fair Employment and Housing Act (FEHA). The EEOC has released an ADA guidance memorandum advising employers to, at a minimum, consider telecommuting as a reasonable accommodation option for certain individuals with disabilities, even if the employer does not have a telecommuting program in place for other employees. It is more likely that telecommuting may be required to accommodate an individual with a disability who can perform quality work at home, particularly when an employer has implemented a telecommuting program to accommodate lifestyles or as a tool to recruit or retain workers. If attendance at work is not an essential function, then working at home becomes a reasonable accommodation. The employer may be expected to set up a home office including an ergonomic chair, desk, computer with special data entry devices and modem.

What You Should Do

Before setting up a telecommuting program, consider first the overall impact on your business and the important issues discussed in the following sections. The questions and issues raised will help you evaluate whether a telecommuting program is right for your company and explain how to set one up and select appropriate employees for the program.

 Where the law has given some direction on a particular issue in the following sections, comments appear in *italics* after the issue is raised.

---

6. *TBG Insurance. Services. Corp. v. Superior Court (Zieminski)*, 96 Cal. App. 4th 443, (2002)

Selection

- Who will decide which employees telecommute?

- If you decide an employee should work from home, does he/she have the choice to refuse and remain in the main office?

- If the employee requests telecommuting, on what basis do you decide to allow or disallow it? *Adopt a systematic approach to telecommuting requests, perhaps by creating a standard request form which you can use to track any inequities in the decision–making process. It might be wise to stay out of the issue of why the employee wants to telecommute altogether, to avoid having to make a value judgment about whether one employee's new baby is more important than another employee's plans to go to law school at night.*

- If the employee's request to work from home is a suggested reasonable accommodation for a disability under the ADA, must you allow it? *The federal courts are split as to whether an employer must grant an employee's request to work at home as a reasonable accommodation.*[7]

- If the employee works from home as a reasonable accommodation under the ADA, do you have an obligation to make reasonable accommodations in the employee's home office (for example, desk to accommodate a wheelchair, special telephone for hearing impairment)? *If the request to work from home is granted as a reasonable accommodation for a disability, you probably have the same obligation to make reasonable accommodations for the employee's home office as you would for the employee's on–site office. However, it would probably not be reasonable to require you to make major structural modifications to the employee's home, such as wheelchair ramps and accessible restrooms.*

Location

- Will the telecommuter work from home each day, or come in to the main office for part of the week?

- How often will he/she be required to report to the main office?

- Will there be a place in the main office that the employee can work?

---

7. *Anzalone v. Allstate Insurance Co.*, 1995 U.S. Dist. LEXIS 588 (E.D. La. Jan. 19, 1995); *Vande Zande v. Wisconsin Dept. of Administration*, 44 F.3d 538, (7th Cir. 1995)

- Is there a place for the telecommuter to park when he/she comes into the main office? Who will be responsible for parking costs? *The California Labor Code requires an employer to reimburse an employee for all money the employee necessarily expends or loses in direct consequence to the performance of his/her duties.*[8] *The employee who normally telecommutes and incurs no parking costs may argue that you must reimburse him/her for those costs when you require the employee to come to the main office.*

Support Staff

- Will the telecommuter have support staff, such as a secretary or assistant? If so, where will the support staff work? If the support staff is in the main office, how will communication between the two be set up?

- How will work get back and forth between the employee and support staff?

Meetings

- Will you require the employee to report to the main office for meetings?

- Can the employee attend some or all of these meetings by teleconference?

- If so, is there a mechanism for getting materials that will be distributed at the meetings to the telecommuter so that he/she can participate fully?

Communicating with Customers/Clients

- When a customer/client calls the employee at the main office number, is there a way to transfer the call to the employee's home? If so, is there a toll or long distance charge for the transferred call? If not, how will the message be forwarded to the employee?

- Will you give the employee's home or home office number to customers/clients?

- Will more calls from the employee's home to the company's customers/clients be long distance than they would be from the main office?

- Will the cost of long distance calls be higher from the employee's home than from the main office, which may have a discount long distance rate due to the high volume of calls?

---

8. Labor Code Section 2802

Turning in Work/Picking Up Projects

- Whose responsibility will it be to get projects from the main office to the employee and back again?

- Will the employee's work deadlines be adjusted in any way to accommodate time necessary to get work back and forth between the two locations?

Supervision and Evaluation

- How will you monitor the employee's production/performance?

- Will you adjust criteria found on most performance evaluations, such as "Interaction with coworkers?"

Company Policies

- Will your policies be changed for telecommuters? For example, will an employee working at home still be required to comply with your dress code specifying "professional attire?"

- How will you monitor employees for compliance with policies, such as those relating to drug and alcohol use on the job?

Employee Family Interaction

- What will your policy be relating to the employee's children or elderly parents needing home care while the employee is working? While an employee obviously cannot be productive while supervising a three–year-old at home, would a teenager coming home from school and doing homework or other activities interfere with the employee's work? What about an elderly parent whose need for care may interfere every few hours?

- Will you have a policy regarding the employee's children helping out by, for example, stuffing envelopes or answering the telephone used for business calls when the employee is away from it momentarily? *Be aware that courts could construe this as a violation of child labor laws.*

Office Equipment and Supplies

- Who will decide what office equipment and supplies the employee needs at home? Will you supply the same type of equipment the employee would have access to in the main office, or less expensive/smaller models? If the equipment you provide for home is older or slower, will that be taken into account when evaluating the employee's productivity?

- Who will be responsible for shopping, transporting and paying for equipment required for a home office? Will the employee be expected to provide items such as a computer, printer, fax, copier, telephone, desk, chair and filing cabinet? If the employee already has a personal computer (or other items) at home, will you require him/her to use it rather than provide another?

- Who will be responsible for shopping, transporting and paying for office supplies, such as, paper, staples and tape?

- If you purchase office supplies, how will the employee get them to his/her home? Will you have them delivered? Will the employee be required to drive to the main office to pick them up?

- If the employee purchases supplies, how and when will you reimburse him/her? It may be more costly to have employees purchase small quantities of supplies rather than your company purchasing them in bulk.

The time an employee spends shopping for office supplies is considered work time for which his/her regular rate of pay is due, including overtime if applicable.

Maintenance

- Who will pay for maintenance and repair of home office equipment? For example, if an employee's computer's modem breaks while he/she is using the computer after hours for personal use, who will be responsible for the repair?

- If the employee is responsible for the repair and cannot afford it for some time, do you have any recourse regarding the hardship this may put on email communication with the employee?

Computer Issues

- Will the employee be allowed to use the company–owned computer you provide for his/her personal use during non–work time?

- Will other members of the household be allowed to use the company–owned computer you provide?

- Is the employee's computer secured by a password or other device?

- Will other members of the household have access to confidential documents?

- How are drafts of confidential computer documents discarded (for example, shredded or simply added to the household trash)?

- Are attacks by computer "viruses" more likely, as computer disks are traded between home and main office?

- Could your company's computer files be wiped out accidentally by a member of the employee's household using the computer for personal use?

Telephone/Fax/Modem

- Who will decide what type of telephone equipment the employee needs at home?

- Will you supply the same type of telephone equipment the employee would have access to in the main office? Many office telephone systems are not compatible with home telephone jacks.

- How many phone lines will the employee need to work from home?

- Will the employee use his/her personal household telephone for work as well as personal calls, or will a line dedicated to business be required? If so, will one line that can be switched over from telephone to fax be sufficient, or will multiple lines be required?

- Will the employee be able to have enough lines run into his/her house? The employee may need to check with his/her local telephone company for the answer to this question.

- Who will be responsible for shopping, transporting and paying for telephone equipment required for a home office?

- Will the employee be expected to provide a telephone and/or an answering machine?

- If the employee already has a second telephone line at home (perhaps for an outside business), will you require him/her to use it rather than provide another?

- Who will pay for maintenance and repair of telephone equipment?

- Who will pay for telephone, fax and modem service charges?

- If the employee uses any of the business lines for personal communication during non–working hours, how will you divide the monthly service charges? Because the employee will be home all day, will the employee be reimbursed for the increased heating and cooling costs for his/her home? Will there be any reimbursement for the employee's increased cost for the electricity required to run his/her computer, monitor, fax, printer, copier and lights in the home office? *The California Labor Code requires an employer to reimburse an employee for all the employee necessarily expends or loses in direct consequence to the performance of his/her duties.*[9]

---

9. Labor Code Section 2802

Miscellaneous Laws

- Will you require the employee working at home to post the required posters and notices that state and federal laws require to be posted in the workplace? *Laws requiring an employer to display a poster contain no exemption for home offices. Therefore, an employee working at home technically should have all the required workplace posters in his/her home office.*

- If an employee works outside the state where your main office is located, how will you monitor and comply with that state's employment laws? *The law in the state in which the employee works is the law that applies to him/her. Therefore, an employee in Nevada working at home for an employer just over the state line in California will be governed by Nevada employment laws.*

- Similarly, for employees working outside the city or county where the main office is located, how will you monitor and comply with local ordinances affecting employment in the employee's location?

- Will the employee need a license or permit to perform industrial homework? *California's Labor Code and the Fair Labor Standards Act (FLSA) regulate certain types of work performed in the home. Although most of these laws are aimed at manufacturing, they may be construed broadly enough to include much of the work done utilizing home technology. If the industrial homework laws apply, permits are required and you have a number of legal responsibilities as an employer of an industrial homeworker.*

City/County Taxes and Licenses

- Cities and counties may not impose business taxes and related licensing requirements on an employee working at home.[10] For purposes of this law, "employee" means a common law employee as reflected in rulings or guidelines used by either the federal Internal Revenue Service or the state Franchise Tax Board.

- Individuals who work at home operating as independent contractors remain subject to city and county taxes and licensing requirements. For more information about the difference between employees and independent contractors, see "Employing Independent Contractors" on page 37.

Wage and Hour Issues

- How will you monitor a non–exempt employee's work hours? Will the employee call the main office to record his/her starting and ending times each day? Will the employee log on to his/her computer, which records starting and ending times via modem to the main office? Will the employee keep a record on paper of

---

10. Business and Professions Code Section 16300

hours worked? *The law does require a record of the hours a non–exempt employee works, including a record of when meal breaks are taken.*[11]

- How will overtime be tracked? How will you control the employee's overtime hours? *You must pay overtime for all overtime hours worked, regardless of whether the employee was authorized to do so, if you knew or had reason to know the overtime was being worked.*[12] *You could argue that you had no knowledge or reason to know an employee was working overtime at home. However, a sudden increase in work completed or an employee's comment that he/she "simply can't get it all done in eight hours (or 40 hours)" could be construed as reason for you to know that the employee was working overtime.*

- How will you know the employee is taking the required meal and break periods?

- How will you know how much meal and break time the employee is taking?

- Will the employee be on an alternative workweek schedule?

- Is the employee part of the rest of his/her "identifiable work unit" working at the main office, or a separate identifiable work unit altogether? *Answer this important question to determine who must participate in the process required to implement an alternative workweek schedule. An identifiable work unit is defined as a "division, department, job classification, shift, separate physical location or a recognized subdivision of any work unit."*[13] *An employee working from home could arguably be an identifiable work unit of one, based on his/her separate physical location, allowing him/her to work a different alternative schedule than the employees in the main office.*

- When is the telecommuting employee's on–call time compensable? *If the employee is free to do whatever he/she chooses at home while waiting for the employer's call to begin work, wages probably are not required for that time.*

- If the employee keeps a written record of hours worked, how will the employee transmit that record to your payroll department?

- When and where will the employee receive his/her paycheck? *California's Labor Code requires employers to post a notice informing employees of the regular time and place of wage payment.*[14] *However, a telecommuting employee who would rather receive his/her paycheck by mail probably could sign an enforceable agreement to that effect.*

- If the employee who normally works at home and has no regular commute must drive to the main office, will the travel time be compensable? *Normally, an employee's regular commute to the workplace is not compensable time. However, since a telecommuting employee does not have a regular commute, he/she could make a plausible argument to the Labor Commissioner that he/she should be compensated for commute time when you require him/her to report to the main office.*

---

11. Labor Code Section 1174
12. IWC Orders Section 3
13. IWC Orders Section 3
14. Labor Code Section 207

- Will you reimburse the employee for mileage? *The California Labor Code requires an employer to reimburse an employee for all money the employee necessarily expends or loses in direct consequence to the performance of his/her duties.*[15] *The employee who normally telecommutes and incurs no commuting costs may have an argument that you must reimburse him/her for mileage when you require the employee to come to the main office.*

- Will the answer to the two previous questions be affected by whether you have requested that the employee come to the main office or whether the choice to come in was the employee's?

- Will you pay an exempt employee on a day where he/she calls the main office to check messages or logs onto the computer for a few minutes to answer an email message from the main office? *Remember, you must pay exempt employees their full salary for **any** day in which they perform any work.*[16]

Workers' Compensation

- How will you determine whether an injury occurred in the course and scope of employment? For example, if the employee injures his/her back while taking out a bag of trash containing discards from both the home–office and the kitchen, was the employee acting within the course of employment?

- Will you effectively be able to fight fraudulent claims when there rarely will be witnesses to an injury?

- Will the employee's inability to physically get away from the work on his/her desk during non–working hours become too stressful? Will the isolation and monotony of being home so much lead to a stress claim?

Safety and Health

- How will you fulfill your duty to provide the employee with a safe and healthy workplace? The U.S. Department of Labor issued a policy statement in February of 2000, that says it will not hold companies responsible for the safety of telecommuting employees' home offices. The directive says the government:

  - Will not inspect employees' home offices, expect employers to inspect them, or hold companies liable for the offices' safety conditions;

  - May pass complaints received from workers about home office safety on to employers but will do no follow–up; and

  - Can hold companies responsible for safety problems with at–home jobs other than office work. For example, jobs such as manufacturing piecework

---

15. Labor Code Section 2802
16. 29 CFR 541.118

involving materials, equipment or work processes that the employer provides or requires to be used in an employee's home. However, even those risky at–home work sites will be inspected only if the government receives complaints.

This directive does not affect your liability under workers' compensation laws for on–the–job injuries in home offices. The directive is available on the U.S. Department of Labor's website at **http://www.osha–slc.gov/OshDoc/ Directive_data/CPL_2–0_125.html**.

- How will you know if the employee is using the safety equipment you provide? (For example, glare screens for computers, wrist rests for keyboards, equipment cord covers.)

- Do you have the right to inspect the employee's home for unsafe conditions? *This question pits the employer's duty to provide a safe workplace directly against the employee's constitutional right to privacy and, to date, no court has squarely addressed this issue.*

- If conditions in the home need adjustments to meet safety standards, who will make and pay for the adjustments?

- Will your Injury and Illness Prevention Plan (IIPP), which is required by law, include items relating to the home office? (For more information on IIPPs, see the California Chamber's **Managing Workers' Comp and Safety in California**. You can order it by calling (800) 331–8877, or visiting the California Chamber store at **http://www.calchamberstore.com**.)

- How will you conduct legally required safety training?

- How will you ensure that the home is a secure place to work? Will you require the employee to keep doors locked and windows closed during working hours and if so, how will you enforce this?

- What is your liability for an incident of violence that occurs in the home during working hours? Will that determination be affected by whether the perpetrator is another member of the household or a stranger?

Relocation

- If the employee moves to a new residence, who will pay the charges to set up new telephone, fax and modem lines?

- Who will pay the cost of moving office equipment and supplies?

Termination

- When the employee quits or is terminated, what provisions have you made for return of equipment, supplies and files?

- How will you transfer work–related computer files from the employee's computer to the main office?

- How will outstanding bills (for example, telephone/fax/modem line) be apportioned?

- If the employee is terminated, will you go to the employee's home to deliver the final wages? *When an employee is terminated, California law specifies that all unpaid wages and accrued but unused vacation are due and payable the same day.*[17]

Employing Home Workers

 Industrial homework is the manufacture of materials or articles in a home for an employer, when such articles or materials are not for the personal use of the employer or a member of his or her family. This type of work includes activity to make, process, prepare, alter, repair or finish, in whole or in part, or to assemble, inspect, wrap or package any articles or materials.

The Law Explained

The Labor Code establishes restrictions on such activities in any room, house, apartment or other premises used, in whole or in part, as a place of dwelling, including outbuildings, such as garages, under the control of the person dwelling on such premises. Both the employer and employee must have necessary permits to perform homework. Articles manufactured in this manner must be labeled, as required by law.

What You Should Do

When employing home workers, you should:

- Comply with all license and permit requirements;

- Limit work to that which can be legally produced by industrial homework;

---

17. Labor Code Section 201

- Comply with all wage, overtime and wage payment laws; and

- Identify all products with required labels or markings.

Employing Foreign Workers

When employing foreign workers, the Immigration Reform and Control Act (IRCA) of 1986, imposes compliance obligations and responsibilities on every employer regardless of size. You are required to verify that an individual is authorized to be employed in the United States. There are civil and criminal penalties for knowingly hiring, referring, recruiting or retaining in employment "unauthorized aliens."

The Law Explained

You must verify that every new hire is either a U.S. citizen or authorized to work in the United States. You must make this verification within three business days after the employee begins work, based on examining documents that evidence identity and employment eligibility. The acceptable documentation is listed on the back of the *I-9 Form*, which you must complete for every employee. For more information, see "Immigration Documents" in Chapter 5, page 114. If you later discover that the employee is an unauthorized alien, you may not continue to employ that person. Similarly, it is unlawful to contract an alien for labor if you know that the alien is unauthorized.

IRCA provides for progressive monetary penalties and cease and desist orders for any person who knowingly hires, recruits or refers for a fee unauthorized aliens. Fines range from $250 to $2,000 for the first offense for each unauthorized alien. You may have to pay up to $10,000 for the third offense for each unauthorized alien. Repeat violators are subject to up to six months in jail for each violation.

You may not require more or different identity and work authorization documents than specified by the United States Citizenship and Immigration Services (USCIS), formerly the Immigration and Naturalization Services (INS) and you must honor documents that appear valid on their face. If an employee has the required verification of eligibility to work, it is illegal to discriminate against him/her on the basis of:

- National origin;

- Citizenship status; or

- Future expiration date of the verifying documents.

If employees are authorized to work but are unable to present the required documentation, you still may hire them. However, employees must give you, within three days of being hired, a receipt demonstrating that they have applied for the required documents and then show you the actual documents within 90 days.

What You Should Do

Have a copy of the *I-9 Form* on hand while reading this section. Each new employee, or his/her translator or preparer, must complete **Section 1** at the time of hire. In any case, the employee must sign this section personally. You must fill out **Section 2** and examine evidence of identity and employment eligibility within three business days after the employee begins work. The acceptable documentation is listed on the back of the *I-9 Form.* If you are shown only one document, it must be on "List A." If it is not on List A, you must instead see one document from "List B" and one document from "List C." Be extremely careful to record the information accurately and on the correct portion of the *I-9 Form.* You may choose to keep photocopies of the documents shown to you, but remember that this does not eliminate the requirement of writing the information on the *I-9 Form* itself. Show the list of acceptable documents on the back of the *I-9 Form* to your employee and allow him/her to choose which verifying documents will be recorded.

You fill out **Section 3** only if updating or reverifying employment eligibility. Reverification is necessary only for expiring work authorization documents, not documents such as a driver's licenses. You must reverify employment eligibility of your employees on or before the expiration date noted in Section 1 of the *I-9 Form.*

Keep completed *I-9 Forms* for all employees in a common file rather than in each employee's personnel file. The forms will then be easily accessible for an audit by immigration or labor officials. This practice also keeps information out of view of managers and supervisors who have no need to know an employee's national origin or immigration status.

The USCIS has available a *Handbook for Employers* (publication #M–274), which you can obtain from your local USCIS office. Look for its listing in your local telephone directory under "Department of Justice" in the U.S. Government listings. You also may order this publication by calling (800) 755–0777 and leaving a message with your name, address and the publication number.

The USCIS Office of Special Counsel has established a toll–free Employer Hotline at (800) 255–8155. The hotline provides prerecorded information about complying with employment–related immigration laws. The hotline also has a fax–on–demand feature that allows callers to enter their fax numbers and quickly receive government forms and information on a variety of subjects. You may also obtain additional information by writing to:

Office of Special Counsel for Immigration Related Unfair Employment Practices
P.O. Box 27728
Washington, DC 20038–7728

 For more information, review the sample *I-9 Form* on the CD that comes with this product.

Employing Leased Workers

An employee leasing arrangement is one in which a staffing company provides employees to an employer for a fee, while handling payroll, benefits, employment taxes and workers' compensation for the leased employees. Some staffing companies hire all or part of an employer's workforce and lease it to the employer. In another arrangement, the staffing company may contract with a client on a long-term basis and place its own employees, including supervisors, at the employer's worksite. In a third situation, the staffing company provides one or more workers on an ongoing basis, but does not manage the operation.

The Law Explained

Although leased workers' compensation, benefits and insurance is provided by the leasing company, the contracting company is potentially liable for each of these benefits if the contracting company is found to be a "joint employer." Joint employment may also affect the contracting company's obligations under its retirement plan. A finding of joint employment depends substantially on the amount of control the contracting company exerts over the leased employees. What's more, in joint employment situations, the combined number of employees of the leasing and contracting companies determines the applicability of specific laws.

> **Example:** The Family and Medical Leave Act (FMLA) applies to companies with 50 or more employees. If the leasing and contracting companies are joint employers with 50 or more combined employees, FMLA will apply to both companies. The contracting company may be required to provide applicable benefits not only to leased employees, but also to qualified members of its own staff.

For more information, see the EEOC's *Application of EEO Laws to Contingent Workers Placed by Temporary Employment Agencies and Other Staffing Firms* at **http://www.eeoc.gov/policy/docs/conting.html**.

Any labor contract for construction, farm labor, garment, janitorial or security guard services must provide compensation sufficient to allow the labor contractor to comply with all applicable laws governing the labor or services to be provided. The contracting party violates the law if it "knows" or "should know" that the terms provide insufficient compensation to allow the contractor to comply. Failure to request or obtain any information from the contractor that is required by any applicable statute, or by the contract or agreement, constitutes knowledge of that information. The law presumes that the contracting party does not violate the law's provisions if the contract is in writing and includes certain specified terms set forth in the law.[18]

What You Should Do

You can minimize joint employer liability by entering into a written contract that includes precautions, such as:

- Specifying that the leasing company is liable for any mistakes it makes, such as payroll tax errors;

- Requiring that the leasing company maintain appropriate insurance coverage and indemnify you for any liability arising out of its administration of the leased employees;

- Insisting on the right to receive information regarding the leasing company's insurance and financial condition;

- Receiving copies of certificates of insurance or coverage declaration pages for each policy that protects the leasing company's workers;

- Checking the leasing company's insurance coverage periodically to be sure that each insurance carrier is licensed in California and is in good standing with the Department of Insurance;

- Avoiding self–insured leasing companies or leasing companies that carry insurance with a large deductible;

- Verifying that the leasing company's financial condition is such that it has the ability to meet obligations for payroll taxes and insurance premiums promptly. As an additional precaution, request an audit report from a reputable accounting firm; and

- Checking with other companies that have used the leasing company in the past to make sure that the company and its principals have the experience necessary to operate a successful employee leasing firm.

---

18. Labor Code Section 2810

Employing Independent Contractors

The true principal/independent contractor relationship offers significant advantages, both to the contractor and to the principal. Contractors enjoy freedom, flexible working conditions, certain tax advantages and the financial and personal rewards of self–employment. Principals benefit from not having to:

- Provide certain statutory employment benefits, such as workers' compensation coverage, unemployment benefits and overtime payments;

- Meet minimum wage obligations; or

- Withhold income taxes from payments for services.

The Law Explained

California administrative agencies and the Internal Revenue Service (IRS) closely scrutinize alleged principal/independent contractor relationships to verify that those relationships are not, in reality, employer/employee relationships. Challenges to the legitimacy of an existing principal/independent contractor relationship may arise in many forms, including:

- Filings for Unemployment Insurance (UI) benefits;

- Claims for unpaid wages;

- Claims for workers' compensation;

- Charges of employment discrimination; and

- Investigations by the IRS and EDD that audit wage payments, workers' compensation coverage and Unemployment Insurance Fund contributions.

 An **independent contractor** is defined as "any person who renders service for a specified recompense for a specified result, under the control of his principal as to the result of his work only and not as to the means by which such result is accomplished."[19]

Many alleged independent contractor relationships fail to pass the legal test when closely examined under both traditional legal criteria and more rigorous tests adopted by the California Supreme Court and labor agencies. The most important factor in that determination involves the independent contractor's right to control the manner and means of accomplishing the desired result, even if the contractor does not exercise that right with respect to all details.

---

19. California Labor Code Section 3353

The consequences you may face for misclassifying an employee as an independent contractor includes significant tax, wage and benefit liabilities, as well as massive fines imposed by the IRS and EDD. You can find extensive information on federal requirements for independent contractor status on the IRS website at ***http://www.irs.ustreas.gov***. Information on state requirements, which vary from federal requirements, may be found on EDD's website at ***http://www.edd.cahwnet.gov***.

What You Should Do

Consider the following questions to determine if you have a true principal/independent contractor relationship:

- Do you have the right to discharge at–will without cause?
- Is the person performing the services engaged in a distinct occupational business?
- Is the work usually done under your close direction or by a specialist without significant supervision by you?
- What are the skills required in the particular occupation?
- Do you or the worker supply the instruments, tools and location for performing the work?
- What is the length of time for which the services are to be performed? Who decides on what schedule it will be done?
- Must the contractor perform the work, or can he/she hire others to do some or all of it?
- Is the method of payment determined by time or by job?
- Is the work part of your regular business? and
- Do either or both parties believe that they are creating the relationship of employer and employee?[20]

Although no single factor is decisive, the right to control the manner and means used clearly is the most important.[21] The *Employment Determination Guide (Form DE 38)*, and a chart entitled *How Six Agencies Determine Independent Contractor-Employee Relationships*, are included on the CD that comes with this product. Use both documents to help determine if you have a true independent contractor relationship.

---

20. *Empire Star Mines Co. v. California Employment Commission*, 28 Cal. 2d 33, 43 (1946)
21. *Barton v. Studebaker Corp. of America*, 46 Cal. App. 707 (1920)

Reporting

All businesses and government agencies must report the hiring of independent contractors to EDD. The report must be filed on the *Report of Independent Contractor(s) (Form DE 542)*, which is included on the CD that comes with this product. You must file the report within 20 days of entering into a contract for, or making payments of, $600 to an independent contractor in any calendar year.[22] For more information, see "Independent Contractors" in Chapter 5, page 123.

What Forms and Checklists Do I Use to Understand My Workforce?

The following table describes forms and checklists associated with understanding and interacting with your workforce.

 You can find these forms on the CD that comes with this product.

Table 4. Required Forms and Checklists

Form/Checklist Name	What do I use it for?	When do I use it?	Who fills it out?	Where does it go?
Application for Permission to Employ Minors in the Entertainment Industry (DLSE-281)	To obtain permission to employ a minor in the entertainment industry	Before minor begins working	Minor's school district fills out and issues the permit	Keep form (permit) on file as long as the minor is employed. Keep it in your personnel records or in a common binder for all minor employees.

---

22. UI Code Section 1088.8

Table 4. Required Forms and Checklists

Form/Checklist Name	What do I use it for?	When do I use it?	Who fills it out?	Where does it go?
Application for Permission to Work in the Entertainment Industry (DLSE-277)	To obtain permission to employ minors in the entertainment industry	Before any minor begins work	You do	In each minor's personnel records
I-9 Form	To verify the immigration status of all employees	**Section 1:** At the time of hire **Section 2:** Within three business days after the employee's first day of work **Section 3:** On or before the expiration date in Section 1	**Section 1:** Employee fills out **Section 2:** You fill out **Section 3:** You fill out if necessary for updating or re-verifying	Keep the forms for all employees in a common file rather than separate personnel records
Permit to Employ and Work (Form B1-4)	To obtain permission to employ a minor	Before the minor begins working (and after the *Statement of Intent to Employ Minor and Request for Work Permit (Form B1-1)* has been approved; see the form's description following in this table)	Minor's school district fills out and issues the permit	Keep form (permit) on file as long as the minor is employed. Keep it in your personnel records or in a common binder for all minor employees.

Table 4. Required Forms and Checklists

Form/Checklist Name	What do I use it for?	When do I use it?	Who fills it out?	Where does it go?
Report of Independent Contractor(s) (Form DE 542)	All new independent contractors 💡 The District Attorney uses the information in this form to locate parents who owe child support funds	As soon as possible after signing the contract	You do	Mail or fax the form to: Employment Development Department P.O. Box 997350 MIC 99 Sacramento, CA 95899-7350 Fax: (916) 255-3211
Statement of Intent to Employ Minor and Request for Work Permit (Form B1-1)	To obtain permission to employ a minor **Note:** Be sure to finish the permit process with the *Permit to Employ and Work (Form B1-4)*, supplied by the minor's school	Before the minor begins working	Each completes the appropriate part: • Minor; • Employer; • Parent; and • School.	File it with the minor's school district. Keep a copy in your personnel records.

Table 5. Recommended Forms and Checklists

Form/Checklist Name	What do I use it for?	When do I use it?	Who fills it out?	Where does it go?
Basic Provisions and Regulations - Child Labor Laws	Understanding limitations when employing minors	When considering employing a minor	NA	NA
Checklist for Employing Minors	Tracking legal issues to consider when hiring a minor	During the recruiting and hiring processes	You do	Keep the checklist in the minor's personnel file
Employment Determination Guide (Form DE 38)	Determining employee versus independent contractor status	During the hiring process	You do	Keep in the applicant's file, or if the applicant is hired, in the personnel file
How Six Agencies Determine Independent Contractor-Employee Relationships	Determining employee versus IC status	During the hiring process	NA	NA

Chapter 3

Recruiting Qualified Applicants

Recruiting employees who will be an asset to your company takes more than just placing an advertisement in the newspaper or posting a job on a website. It takes preparation, including:

- Determining what the job is and the qualities a candidate must have to be successful;

- Identifying resources where you are most likely to find such candidates;

- Preparing a marketing strategy that qualified candidate respond to; and

- Making smart choices when you make a hiring decision.

Certainly some jobs are easier to fill than others, but even those positions are worth the effort to properly prepare. Consider how much time you spend training new employees, or how much expense you may face if a bad choice result in a workers' compensation claim, a discrimination charge or a wrongful discharge law suit.

This chapter takes you through the first step of finding the "right employee" by helping you define the job, write the job specification and classify the job as exempt or non-exempt. You can also use the *Pre-Hire Checklist* on the CD that comes with this product to help organize the process of finding and preparing to hire an employee.

Describing the Job

The starting point for recruiting employees is to understand and identify the job or jobs to be performed. Without this information, the recruiter or manager wastes both time and money in the recruiting process. Worse yet, the selected applicant will either be (1) ill equipped for the job, requiring extended training and having a greater likelihood of failure, or (2) overqualified for the job and more likely to be bored and move on quickly thus wasting your efforts. If you don't have a job description, create one. Every position in your organization should have a job description.

The Law Explained

There are no legal requirements that you have job descriptions or, if you do have them, what they should contain or how they should be formatted. Perhaps the most important purpose of a job description is to identify the essential functions of the position.

 According to the Equal Employment Opportunity Commission (EEOC), **essential functions** are those tasks or functions of a particular position that are fundamental to the position (as opposed to marginal).

The Americans with Disabilities Act (ADA) of 1990, from which the issue of essential functions has come into focus, accepts several reasons why a function could be considered essential, including:

- The position exists to perform the function. For example, if you hire someone to proofread documents, the ability to proofread accurately is an essential function, because this is why the position exists;

- There are a limited number of other employees available to perform the function, or among whom the function can be distributed. For example, it may be an essential function for a file clerk to answer the telephone in a company with only three employees, where each employee has to perform many different tasks; or

- A function is highly specialized and the person in the position is hired for his/her special expertise or ability to perform it.

Example: A company expanding its business in Japan is hiring a new salesperson, so it requires someone with not only sales experience, but also with the ability to communicate fluently Japanese.

Knowing the essential functions of the job aids you in:

- Writing appropriate interview questions;

- Determining whether a person is qualified to perform the essential functions; and

- Identifying reasonable accommodations to enable a disabled person to perform the essential functions.

In addition, a properly developed job description sets forth the uniformly expected physical and mental demands, the educational prerequisites and the experiential expectations for candidates. These predefined standards may be cited to defend your hiring decisions from claims of discrimination.

Disability discrimination laws do not limit your ability to establish or change the content, nature, or functions of the job. You have the right to establish what a job is and what functions are required to perform it. The laws simply require that the qualifications of an individual with a disability are evaluated in relation to the job's essential functions.

What You Should Do

Create effective job descriptions that provide your executives, managers, supervisors and employees with a clear understanding and appreciation for the how each job fits into your company overall and contributes to the achievement of the company's mission. Doing this provides guidance for all levels of employees in matters relating to:

- Hiring;

- Reporting relationships;

- Performance expectations;

- Compensation; and

- Career opportunities.

Why You Need Job Descriptions and What They Contain

Job descriptions clearly set forth job duties and expectations by:

- Taking the uncertainty out of differentiating the expectations and requirements of various jobs;

- Minimizing employee discontent associated with pay differentials between jobs;

- Clarifying the role of the job and the expectations for the persons performing the job;

- Guiding initial training and forming a foundation for an agreement between management and employees as to the expected outcomes; and

- Supporting the performance evaluation process. Where performance fails to meet expectations, the job description provides direction for further training. Moreover, where widespread performance deficiencies are observed, job descriptions provide a focus for identifying organizational weaknesses.

Job descriptions are the basis for job evaluation to determine compensation systems and compensation levels. They are the starting point for analyzing the functions of each job and determining the relative "value" of the position within the company and the job market.

From a defensive viewpoint, job descriptions provides clear, written recruiting guidelines and performance expectations needed to defend claims of discrimination in the hiring and promotion process and a clear understanding of the job's scope and nature. By using the job description, both the recruiter and potential employees can have a clear understanding of the job during the interview. This practice allows candidates to determine whether the job is right for them and helps them understand where personal deficiencies may limit their employability—both of which may save the organization valuable time and resources and, perhaps, litigation exposure.

Well written job descriptions provide the company with solid legal backing with respect to any decisions that must be made about jobs and people. They are invaluable in defending wrongful termination lawsuits and are decision guides when faced with reorganizations or reductions in force. For more information, see Chapter 7, "Conducting Reorganizations and Workforce Reductions."

The following discussion of the components of a job description can help you write a job description for positions in your company. Each of the components is designed to contribute to an overall picture of the requirements for and expectations of the person needed to fill the position.

Job Title

This is the name you use to identify the job. Often it may be the last thing you decide upon, as the exercise of preparing the job description may guide you to the selection of an appropriate job title. If you are adding a new function to an existing job, the new job title may be the same as a previous one, only designating it as a higher level. For example, "Clerk II" or "Senior Mechanic."

Summary

Like the job title, the summary is often left for last as it should be a one or two paragraph capsule of the essential functions and reporting relationships.

Essential Functions

The key factor in determining whether you need to equally consider qualified disabled persons for job openings and promotions is whether the disabled person can perform the "essential functions" of the job. A job function may be considered essential if it constitutes the fundamental job duties of the position, or if the reason the job exists is to perform that function.

The essential functions component is the heart of the job description. In identifying essential functions, be sure to consider (1) whether employees in the position actually are required to perform the function and (2) whether removing that function would fundamentally change the job.

To identify the essential functions of the job, first identify the purpose of the job and the importance of actual job activities in achieving this purpose. In evaluating the importance of job functions, consider, among other things, the:

- Frequency with which a function is performed;

- Amount of time spent on the function; and

- Consequences if the function is not performed.

The EEOC considers various forms of evidence to determine whether or not a particular function is essential; these include, but are not limited to the:

- Employer's judgment;

- Amount of time spent on the job performing that function; and

- Availability of others in the department to fill in for the person who performs that function.

It is imperative that you determine the essential functions of a job, both as the criteria for deciding the ability of the disabled person to perform the job and as a defense against any subsequent claim of discrimination. To determine if a function is essential, give consideration to, at minimum, the following factors:

- Does the job exist to perform this function?

- Who else is available to perform this function?

- What level of expertise or skill is required to perform this function?

- What is the experience of previous or current employees in this job?

- What is the amount of time spent performing this function?

- What are the consequences of failing to perform this function? and

- What is stated in the job description and employment advertisements?

Because determining essential functions is one of the least clear provisions of the disability discrimination laws, you should, as a matter of policy, take the following steps in making a determination:

1. **Document all important job functions** — Maintain current detailed job descriptions that set forth essential functions for each position;

2. **Be accurate and realistic** — Job descriptions or definitions should describe the actual duties of the position rather than the "ideal" set of duties. Individuals who inflate their importance to the company may exaggerate the extent of their duties or those of their subordinates and are not a reliable source for a description of essential job functions. Job descriptions that are easily called into question by those who know the workplace are of little or no value;

3. **Stay current** — Many jobs change rapidly. Review and update job descriptions periodically to ensure accuracy;

4. **Be flexible** — Flexibility is important when describing the essential functions of a job. Tasks that can transfer easily to another person and are not necessarily the heart of a job, are unlikely to constitute essential functions. Employers who are able to pare their job descriptions down to the core functions are more likely to prevail in litigation than are those who insist that every traditional function of a job is essential;

5. **Review job descriptions with employees** — It is always a good idea for you to know what employees are actually doing and for employees to understand exactly what is expected of them. Review the essential functions of a job with employees to solicit their input and increase accuracy; and

6. **Document agreement** — After employees review the essential functions of their position(s), document that the employees reviewed and agreed with the description of essential job functions.

To help identify essential functions, use action words to describe an activity. Also, distinguish between methods and results. For example, is the essential function *moving* a fifty pound box from place to another, or is it *carrying* the box to a new location? Essential functions often do not need to be performed in one particular manner (unless doing otherwise would create an undue hardship). However, if they must be, identify these essential functions as such because this unique requirement may impact the determination of reasonable accommodations.

Physical Requirements

Keeping in mind the requirements of the ADA and FEHA, it is important to identify the essential physical requirements of the job. Describe this component in terms of the physical activity and degree of strength, flexibility and agility required and the frequency and duration with which the effort must be exerted.

Knowledge, Skill and Experience

List all of the knowledge, skills and experience necessary to perform the job. You may wish to divide these components into requirements and preferences, as certain attributes may be absolutely required for a particular job, while other attributes may be desirable but not necessary. For example, a nursing degree for a medical case manager may be required, while an electrical engineering degree for a supervising electrician might be desirable. Except where absolutely necessary, avoid strict requirements that may prevent you from considering qualified candidates. For example, you may be willing to substitute a bachelor's degree in finance plus 10 years of professional experience for a master's degree in finance.

The requirements listed on the job description must support the essential functions and serve as the primary criteria for selecting/rejecting candidates. Keep in mind that, under the ADA, you cannot refuse to hire a qualified candidate who meets the requirements and whose disability can be reasonably accommodated.

Reporting Relationships

Each job has an important place in the organization and a thorough understanding of that place by the incumbent as well as by those who have contact with him/her is important. The job description should identify the position's place in the organization's chain of command, including the position(s) to which it reports, as well as the position(s) that report(s) to it.

Career Path

In addition to detailing the reporting relationships, many job descriptions include a statement of the career paths, if any, to which the position may lead. This is useful support for the goal setting portion of performance review and evaluation. For more information, see Chapter 6, "Evaluating Employee Performance.

Financial Responsibility

Where the position has responsibility for a profit or cost center, some companies prefer to quantify the extent of that responsibility. This aids the recruiter in evaluating the candidate's previous level of responsibility and clearly defines the expectations for the candidate or incumbent.

Compensation Category

The compensation information gathered for the job description aids in determining whether the position is likely to be exempt or non-exempt. However, this decision should be confirmed by further analysis using the tools provided in "Determining Exempt or Non-Exempt Status" in Chapter 4, page 84.

 Use the new *Job Description Template* on the CD that comes with this product to develop your company's job descriptions.

Job Description Software

Although it is possible to sit down with pen and paper to describe each job in your workplace, using computer software can make the task much easier. Writing job descriptions is not as difficult as it sounds with the help of a California Chamber software package called **Descriptions Now!**™. The software contains complete information on how to write job descriptions, as well as 3,000 sample descriptions to help make your task less challenging. **Descriptions Now!** is available from the California Chamber by calling (800) 331–8877, or visiting the California Chamber store at ***http://www.calchamberstore.com***.

Preparing the Job Specification

Once you have the job description completed, prepare a job specification, which is really a modified version of the job description omitting the detail about the job. It provides guidance to whomever writes the copy for the advertisement, job posting, flyer, radio spot or other job marketing tool. The job specification includes:

- Job title;
- To whom the position reports;
- Summary of the position;
- Educational requirements;
- Desired experience;
- Required specialized skills or knowledge;
- Physical or other special requirements associated with the job;
- Any occupational hazards;

- Salary range; and

- Benefits.

 Use the new *Job Specification Template* on the CD that comes with this product to help you develop job specifications.

Identifying Sources for Applicants

Once you have clearly identified the job and the qualities you are seeking, it is time to market the position. As with all marketing campaigns, the goal should be to get the best return on the dollars you invest. This means devising a strategy that is most likely to yield both the best quality and quantity of candidates.

Internal Job Posting

Some employers are required by union contracts or internal policies to post notices of job openings to their current workforce. Whether or not you are required to do so, this method of advertising is a good source for getting new candidates. Posting the job internally also encourages your current employees to recommend your company to people they know. You may want to consider offering cash bonuses or other rewards for referrals that result in hiring, particularly for hard–to–fill positions.

Take caution if the current workforce appears to exclude certain minorities that are represented in your community, or is predominantly male where female employees could fill positions. In such cases, relying on the current workforce entirely for new employees can get you in trouble by perpetuating the exclusion of minorities or women.

Word Of Mouth

Tell everyone you know — friends, neighbors, professional associates, customers, vendors, colleagues from associations — that you have a job opening. Someone might know the perfect candidate. Networking is one of the best ways to find a job candidate.

Recruiting and Placement Agencies

These companies are in the business of placing qualified candidates for which you pay a fee. Some agencies are hired on a retainer basis and charge a flat fee per placement. Others operate on a contingent basis, such as successful candidate placement and charge a fee that is usually related to the salary offered to the candidate they represent. If you are considering using an agency, review its contract carefully to be sure you know precisely what services it provides and what you will pay.

Job Match Service

You can let your tax dollars work for you by contacting the Employment Development Department (EDD) to help you find employees. EDD provides free job services to both employers and job seekers. List your job openings in EDD's Job Match system and let the Department refer qualified applicants to you free of charge. The telephone number for your local EDD office is located in the state government section of your local telephone directory under "Employment Development Department."

Educational Institutions

Consider listing your openings with appropriate universities, colleges, trade and vocational schools. Local school districts often have job training and placement programs for high schools students. Get to know the placement counselors and teachers who train these future employees who your company needs and ask them to keep you in mind when they have a student who excels in an area that fits within your company.

Complex federal and state rules apply to the employment of minors. For more information, see "Employing Minors" in Chapter 2, page 15.

Newspapers

Newspaper want ads are the tried and true means of finding employees. They can be an inexpensive way of getting the word out to the general population. Don't ignore smaller, community-based newspapers as well, particularly if you are seeking to fill relatively low paid positions to which people are unlikely to commute long distances.

Magazines

Trade association newsletters, professional journals and industry publications often have classified ad sections where you can advertise job openings. This is an effective way to attract skilled people in a particular industry or profession.

Radio and Television

These are expensive ways to advertise for employees, but may be justified in cases of mass hiring for new business or relocations. Radio can be useful for reaching the target market of a particular station and cable television can often be cost efficient for reaching large numbers of a targeted audience.

Internet

There are a variety of online job websites that allow employers to post openings. Some are specialized and target certain skills and professions. Potential employees from all over the world can search these databases, so be prepared to receive and screen lots of applications.

If your company has a website, add a jobs page where you can post open positions and accept applications and/or resumes from candidates using an online application, email, fax or traditional mail.

Members of the California Chamber can access Internet recruiting sources by visiting our website at ***http://www.hrcalifornia.com*** and clicking the "Hiring Center" link.

Job Banks

Many professional associations have job banks for their members. Contact groups related to your industry, even if they are located outside of your local area and ask them to alert their members to your staffing needs.

Foreign Recruiting

Some employers have found it necessary to go beyond the borders of the United States to find certain skills because of a shortage of trained personnel in certain industries and jobs. For more information, see "Employing Foreign Workers" in Chapter 2, page 33.

Other Community Sources

Post notices at senior citizen centers and other places where potential employees congregate. Retirees who need extra income or a productive way to fill their time can make excellent employees. Talk to other businesses with which you are friendly. They may have just finished a recruiting effort and have more valuable applicants than they could employ.

Advertising the Job

When advertising a position, consider two important aspects of any proposed advertisement:

1. Does it avoid reference to a secure contract that would contradict an at–will employment relationship? See "Employment At–Will" in Chapter 2, page 13; and

2. Does it comply with all state and federal discrimination laws?

Avoiding Discrimination in Job Advertisements

When drafting a help–wanted advertisement, avoid language indicating limitations or exclusions on the basis of race, color, national origin, religion, sex, age, marital status, sexual orientation, or disability. See the following table for examples of appropriate and inappropriate terms and phrases. For more information on language that should be avoided in job advertisements, see the sample *Watch Your Language!!* form on the CD that comes with this product.

Table 6. Language in Job Advertisements

Do use:	Don't use:
Enthusiastic salesperson	Young and energetic salesman
Food server	Waitress
Repair person	Repairman
Travel required	Perfect for a single person willing to travel

You may use words such as "mature" or "experienced," as they do not discriminate against those protected by age discrimination laws.

 If pictures or drawings of people are a part of an advertisement, be sure to include minorities, women and people with disabilities.

New for 2004 Although extremely rare, no discrimination will be found if otherwise prohibited language is used where it identifies a bona fide occupational qualification (BFOQ). The use of sex as a BFOQ was made even rarer when California passed a law outlawing discrimination based on gender or gender identity.[1]

The law defines **gender** as a person's "identity, appearance, or behavior whether or not that identity, appearance or behavior is different from that traditionally associated with the person's sex at birth." So, for example, advertising for a male model for a men's clothing photo shoot may no longer qualify as a BFOQ.

Complying with Affirmative Action Requirements

Affirmative action program requirements impose on some employers the duty to take positive steps to identify discrimination based on protected class status and to improve work opportunities for women, racial and ethnic minorities and persons belonging to other protected groups who have been deprived of job opportunities. These requirements most often result from an employer's contracts with federal, state and local governments.

However, California voters approved Proposition 209 in 1996, barring state and local governments (but not the federal government) from granting preferential treatment to any individual or group on the basis of race, sex, ethnicity, or national origin in the operation of government hiring, contracting and education. Employers with affirmative action plans, as a result of state or local government contracts, should contact legal counsel for the most current information about the status of the law.

Proposition 209 is a state measure and in no way affects federal affirmative action programs. Therefore, employers with federal contracts subject to affirmative action requirements must remain in compliance with those requirements.

---

1. Government Code section 12940

Maintaining Equal Employment Opportunity Data

Many employers are required to maintain records relating to their recruiting, hiring and employment activities to satisfy the requirements of Title VII of the Civil Rights Act of 1964.

The Law Explained

Employers who have 15 or more employees, must maintain a record of the sex, race and national origin of applicants and employees apart from personnel files.[2] Maintain these records to demonstrate, if necessary, that you are attempting to recruit and develop a workforce reflective of the community's ethnic profile. Keep Equal Employment Opportunity (EEO) records in a common file rather than in each employee's personnel file.

Annual filing of Standard Form 100 (*EEO-1*) is required of:

- All private employers with 100 or more employees, who are subject to Title VII of the Civil Rights Act of 1964 (as amended by the Equal Employment Opportunity Act of 1972);

- Primary and secondary school systems;

- Institutions of higher education;

- Indian tribes; and

- Tax–exempt private membership clubs other than labor organizations.

You are also required to file if:

- You have fewer than 100 employees;

- Your company is owned or affiliated with another company; or

- There is centralized ownership, control or management (such as central control of personnel policies and labor relations), so that the group legally constitutes a single enterprise and the entire enterprise employs a total of 100 or more employees.

Form *EEO-1* also must be filed by most federal contractors (private employers), who:

- Have 50 or more employees;

- Are prime contractors or first–tier subcontractors and have a contract, subcontract, or purchase order amounting to $50,000 or more;

---

2. 42 U.S.C. 2000e–8(c)

- Serve as a depository of Government funds in any amount; or

- Are financial institutions that are issuing and paying agents for U.S. Savings Bonds.

New for 2004 The EEOC has implemented new filing requirements for form *EEO–1* effective for the filing deadline of September 30, 2003 and September 30 of subsequent years. The new reporting system is entirely on the EEOC's website at **www.eeoc.gov/eeo1survey/**, where you can access to up to 10 years of your company's historical information. Completing and filing form *EEO–1* online is convenient because the website contains all the instructions and forms needed.

 No paper version of form *EEO-1* is available. You must file it on the EEOC's website.

If you are a first time filer, the EEOC website has a simple registration form. On its website, the EEOC will issue you a company number and you then can log into the reporting system to complete form *EEO–1*. If you've filed a form *EEO–1* in previous years, some information on the online form will pre–fill from the previous year. The online reporting system uses encrypted files for data transfer to ensure data privacy and security.

You can obtain more information by visiting the website or contacting the EEOC at:

EEO–1 Joint Reporting Committee
P.O. Box 19100
Washington, D.C. 20036–9100
Phone: 1–866–286–6440
TTY: 202–663–7184
Fax: 202–663–7185
Email: e1.techassistance@eeoc.gov

What You Should Do

Use the *Equal Employment Opportunity Data* form on the CD that comes with this product to collect the necessary data. Give this form to each applicant to fill out along with a job application, but separate it from the job application before the application is passed on to the person doing the interviewing or hiring. Applicants must be informed that completing this data is entirely voluntary and will not affect their applications for employment.

The data you keep for statistical purposes should include only:

- Name;

- Sex;

- Race; and

- EEO–1 category.

The EEOC has nine categories of job classifications, which are described on the sample *EEOC Job Categories* chart on the CD that comes with this product. Classify all employees by the category that most closely matches their job duties.

Keep all EEO records in a common file, separate from individual personnel files.

For more information, contact your local office of the DFEH, listed in your local telephone directory under "Fair Employment and Housing" in the State Government section or contact the EEOC at:

Equal Employment Opportunity Commission
901 Market Street, #500
San Francisco, CA 94103
(415) 356–5100
www.eeoc.gov

Obtaining Information

You may obtain the information necessary for completing form *EEO–1* either by:

- Examining your workforce visually; or

- Maintaining post–employment records regarding the identity of employees for the sole purpose of completing the report. For more information, see "Retaining Records" on page 59.

Reporting Employment Figures

The employment figures you report on form *EEO-1* may come from any pay period in the third quarter: July through September. Employers who have been granted permission to use year–end employment figures in the past may still do so.

Requesting an Extension

To request an extension of the time to file your annual report, submit an email to e1.techassistance@eeoc.gov before September 30. In the email, include your company name, company number, address and the contact information for the person responsible for the report.

Retaining Records

You must retain recruitment and hiring records for at least one year from the date the record was made or the personnel action occurred, whichever occurs later. This includes:

- Requests for reasonable accommodation;

- Application forms submitted by applicants; and

- Other records having to do with hiring, promotion, demotion, transfer, lay–off or termination, rates of pay or other terms of compensation and selection for training or apprenticeship.

Involuntary Terminations Records

Records of involuntary terminations must be kept for at least one year from the date of termination. Where a charge of discrimination has been filed, you must preserve all personnel records relevant to the charge or action until final disposition of the charge or the action.

Permanent Records

Permanent records related to the racial or ethnic identity of an employee must be kept separately from the employee's basic personnel record, or any other records available to those responsible for personnel decisions.

Using Employment Applications

Using the sample *Employment Application - Long Form* and sample *Employment Application - Short Form* on the CD that comes with this product allows you to gather a great deal of pertinent job applicant information without creating liability for discrimination. They have been reviewed thoroughly to ensure that all questions are acceptable under the equal employment laws. The long form requests more information than the short form does about the applicant's availability, language and other skills, licensing and/or certification, employment history and military service. You may choose to use one form only or alternate between the forms, depending on how much information you need from applicants for different positions.

The Law Explained

Although you are not required by law to use a formal employment application, we recommend that every candidate fill one out. Even if you received a resume from a candidate, an application form should still be supplied and completed. An application is a simple method of collecting information about a potential employee's experience, skills, training and limitations. Do not consider resumes, which often arrive unsolicited, requests for employment. Although resumes are helpful tools, they often do not contain the range of information that may be revealed by the completion of a standardized employment application.

In addition to its role in gathering information, an application can be designed for damage control in anticipation of the possibility that an applicant/employee may later sue you for such things as wrongful termination, defamation, or invasion of privacy. Because resumes are prepared by applicants, they do not contain the legal protections incorporated in a properly designed employment application. Unsolicited resumes are not considered employment applications for the purposes of equal employment data. At the time of this writing, the EEOC is considering new rules concerning when a job application received over the Internet qualifies as an application for record keeping purposes. For more information about this matter, see ***http:// edocket.access.gpo.gov/2004/04-4090.htm***.

Retention requirements vary among the laws pertaining to job applications. See "Records Retention" in Chapter 1, page 5 for a discussion of what records must be kept and for how long. A good rule is simply to keep job applications of those who are not hired for at least two years. Keep applications from those who are hired for the duration of employment, plus two years. You are not required to keep unsolicited resumes or applications.

What You Should Do

Carefully compare any application you're currently using with the sample *Guide for Pre-Employment Inquiries*, *Employment Application - Long Form* and *Employment Application - Short Form* on the CD that comes with this product. The *Guide for Pre-Employment Inquiries* contains 19 categories of potentially discriminatory questions, as well as examples of what is prohibited and what is acceptable. This list applies to all pre-employment inquiries, whether made:

- On a job application;

- In an interview; or

- During an informal lunch with an applicant.

Be especially careful about using applications that are drafted and printed in another state (for example, where your company is headquartered) unless they are reviewed with particular caution for compliance with California laws.

To maximize your protection, be sure your employment application includes the following "damage–control" provisions:

- An authorization to check all references listed by the applicant. Because you may be liable for negligent hiring if you fail to check an applicant's references, this damage–control provision helps protect you from a claim that the applicant's privacy was invaded. Obtaining information from former employers is easier if they are aware that their former employee has authorized disclosure to you. Be aware, however, that this release cannot protect you against claims of intentional misconduct or employment discrimination, such as deliberately asking a former employer for protected information, such as medical history or marital status;

- A statement that all answers given by the applicant are true and any omissions or false information are grounds for rejection of the application or for termination. Recent court decisions have allowed employers to use an applicant's placement of false information on a job application as evidence in their defense of wrongful termination lawsuits, even when the employer did not discover the information was false until after the employee was terminated;

- An initial statement that any future employment will be on an at–will basis. This clause helps to preserve the presumption that employment is at–will and states that any contrary representations must be contained in a signed, written document to become binding.

- As required by California law, an explanation and a check box on your job application advising applicants that you may conduct a review of certain public records and their rights with regard to the use of those records.

Have the applicant initial each of the "damage–control" provisions separately in spaces provided in the margin of the application. By drawing attention to these important provisions, it's less likely that applicants will later be able to claim successfully that they were not made aware of what they were signing. Although not foolproof, such provisions may keep you out of court or tip the balance of evidence in your favor once there.

Some employers send unsolicited resumes back to the applicant along with a note explaining that there currently are no openings for the position sought. On the other hand, you may decide to keep the unsolicited applications and resumes in a separate folder as a pool of potential employees.

If you talk to applicants at the time they give you their completed applications, you may be tempted to jot down a few things in the margins of the applications. Resist that temptation unless your notes meet the tough tests of being completely legible and not open to any misinterpretation and do not touch upon any of the protected classes. For more information about protected classes, see "The Law Explained" in Chapter 4, page 65. If you feel you must make some notes, be sure that they are brief, clear and legible. Do not use a coded rating system that could be misinterpreted in the future.

> **Example:** Notations in the margin of an application may seem insignificant at first. However, consider the following real–life scenario: An employer made a notation on the application of a candidate for a position at the jewelry counter of a large department store. Although he intended the notation to mean "no experience selling jewelry," the words "no jew" resulted in the applicant filing religious discrimination charges against the store.

What Forms and Checklists Do I Use to Recruit Qualified Applicants?

The following table describes forms and checklists associated with recruiting qualified applicants.

 You can find these forms on the CD that comes with this product.

Table 7. Recommended Forms and Checklists

Form/Checklist Name	What do I use it for?	When do I use it?	Who fills it out?	Where does it go?
EEOC Job Categories	To determine appropriate EEO classification for new or existing jobs	When filling out *EEO-1* form	You	NA
Employment Application - Long Form	Gathering key work history information from an applicant, obtaining authorization to check references and background and certification that all information is truthful	During the recruiting process	Applicant	Keep in the employee's personnel file, if the applicant is hired.

If you don't hire the applicant, keep the paperwork for two years. |
| *Employment Application - Short Form* | Gathering key work history information from an applicant, obtaining authorization to check references and background and certification that all information is truthful | During the recruiting process | Applicant | Keep in the employee's personnel file, if the applicant is hired.

If you don't hire the applicant, keep the paperwork for two years. |
| *Equal Employment Opportunity Data* | To collect EEO data on applicants | When accepting an employment application | Applicant | EEO data file |

Table 7. Recommended Forms and Checklists

Form/Checklist Name	What do I use it for?	When do I use it?	Who fills it out?	Where does it go?
Guide for Pre-Employment Inquiries	Outlining what you can and can't ask during the recruiting process	During the recruiting process	No filling out needed; use as a reference	NA
Job Description	To create a job description	During initial preparation or revision of job descriptions	Manager, supervisor or HR	Job description file or employee personnel file
Job Specification-Requisition	To describe minimum job requirements	When preparing to recruit for and advertise a job	Manager, supervisor or HR	Recruitment file
Pre-Hire Checklist	To help organize the process of recruiting employees	During the recruiting process	No filling out needed	NA
Watch Your Language!!	As a guide for interviewers	When preparing to interview job applicants	NA	NA

Chapter 4

Interviewing and Selecting Qualified Employees

If you followed the advice in Chapter 3, you should now have a bundle of applications from candidates who meet the specifications of the job you need to fill. What you do with those applications determines whether you (1) make a hiring decision that is likely to yield a successful, competent employee and (2) keep your company out of trouble by making non–discriminatory hiring decisions.

Interviewing Applicants

To ensure that the interviews you conduct do not expose you to lawsuits, create a list of acceptable interview questions and stick to them. The sample *Employment Interview Checklist* on the CD that comes with this product contains such a list. You may choose to ask all of the listed questions or only those you feel pertain to a particular job. You also may develop your own questions, but be sure that they are strictly job–related, non–discriminatory and not an invasion of the applicant's privacy.

The Law Explained

There is no specific process required by law for selecting employees. The law does require, however, that whatever process you use does not exclude candidates for unlawful reasons. Just about everyone is a member of some class that is protected by state or federal prohibitions on employment discrimination. Protected classes include:

- Race/color;

- National origin/ancestry;

- Sex (including gender)

- Religion;

- Age (for persons 40 and older);

- Mental or physical disability;

- Veteran status;

- Medical condition (including genetic characteristics);

- Marital status;

- Sexual orientation; and

- Pregnancy.

FEHA protects not only *actual* membership in the classes specified in the FEHA, but also *perceived* membership in one or more of those classes.

Example: An individual could file a sexual orientation discrimination charge, claiming that he was discriminated against because he was perceived as homosexual, even if he was not in fact homosexual.

In addition, a person is protected by the FEHA if he/she is associated with a person who has, or is perceived to have, any of the FEHA's protected characteristics. For example, a black female employee could file a charge of discrimination claiming she was fired because she married a white man.

Disability Discrimination

Avoiding disability discrimination claims presents, perhaps, the greatest challenge to employers. California's discrimination laws often are more stringent than those of other states. California's FEHA gives employees more protection than they have under the federal vs.ADA. The U.S. Supreme Court said the benchmark test for being "substantially limited in a major life activity" under the ADA, means an individual must have an impairment that prevents or severely restricts activities that are of central importance to most people's daily lives, rather than just to a particular job.[1] Under California disability protection laws, employment–related activities are specifically included.

Some of the most important differences in disability discrimination laws for California employers include:

- Broadening the definition of "disability";

- Eliminating mitigating measures (such as medications or eyeglasses) when determining whether an individual is disabled;

- Requiring only that a disability "limit" a major life activity, rather than "substantially limit" it;

---

1. *Toyota Motor Mfg, Kentucky, Inc. v. Williams*, 534 U.S. 184 (2002)

- Limiting medical and psychological examinations and disability–related inquiries for both applicants and employees;

- Mandating that an employer engage in a good–faith, timely, interactive process to determine reasonable accommodations; and

- Including employers with as few as five employees while the federal ADA includes employers of 15 or more employees.

Discrimination laws also contain very specific requirements regarding reasonable accommodations for all persons with disabilities. Many standard job applications contain inquiries prohibited under the disability discrimination laws, such as: "Do you have a health condition that may prevent you from performing the job for which you are applying?" This seemingly innocent question fails the test because it does not allow for an applicant who can perform the essential functions of the job with reasonable accommodation. California law prohibits an employer at the pre–offer stage from:

- Requiring any medical or psychological examination of an applicant;

- Inquiring as to whether an applicant has a mental or physical disability, or medical condition;

- Asking about the nature or severity of a mental disability, physical disability, or medical condition; or

- Inquiring about an applicant's workers' compensation history.

Neither increases in workers' compensation premiums nor medical benefit costs constitute a legitimate basis for denying a job opportunity to a qualified disabled person. However, at the pre–offer stage, an employer *is* permitted to:

- Inquire into the ability of an applicant to perform job–related functions; and

- Respond to an applicant's request for reasonable accommodation.

New for 2004 FEHA contains a specific provision that clearly provides that an employee or applicant is not qualified if a disability poses a direct threat to his or her own health or safety.[2] The EEOC's regulations on the ADA contain the same provision. The U.S. Supreme Court upheld that interpretation of the ADA when it ruled that a job applicant would not be a "qualified individual" under ADA if the essential duties of the job would pose a direct threat to his/her own health or safety.[3] The Supreme Court sent the case back to the 9th Circuit Court to determine whether the company's rejection was based on a sufficient "individualized medical assessment of the risks." The 9th Circuit Court then said that the ADA requires more than "the advice of a generalist and an expert in preventive medicine" to conclude that the individual's

---

2. Government Code Section 12940(a)(1)
3. *Chevron U.S.A. v. Echazabal* 122 S. Ct. 2045 (2002)

medical condition met the "direct threat" requirements. As of this writing, the case has been returned to the federal district court for further analysis of the evidence.[4]

Due to potential liability under the ADA, as well as California's FEHA, it is wise to familiarize yourself with the basic requirements of those laws before interviewing job applicants. Although it may seem only natural to ask certain questions of an interviewee whose physical disability is obvious to you, you may discover that many of those questions are strictly prohibited.

The EEOC has prepared guidelines for the types of disability–related pre–employment questions an employer may and may not ask of a job applicant under the ADA. The guidelines also address the effect of the ADA on medical examinations given to applicants and employees. Copies of the guidelines are available on the EEOC website at ***http://www.eeoc.gov/policy/guidance.html*** or may be obtained by written request for notice number 915.002 (7/27/00) at the following address:

Equal Employment Opportunity Commission
901 Market Street, #500
San Francisco, CA 94103
Attention: Intake Department

Other Issues to Avoid

Become familiar with the *Guide for Pre-Employment Inquiries* on the CD that comes with this product, which outlines discriminatory and acceptable interview topics. During interviews or other pre–employment contact, do not ask questions about marital status or children.

> **Example:** You may not ask an applicant if she is pregnant, has children, or is planning to have them. If you know an applicant has children, you may not ask whether he/she has made provisions for childcare. Similarly, if you would not ask a question of a man, do not ask it of a woman. For example, "If you became pregnant, how much time would you need away from work?"

Be careful when asking about hobbies or outside activities. It is discriminatory to ask about clubs, societies, lodges, or organizations to which the applicant belongs that might indicate race, religion, national origin, sex, age, etc. Don't ask about what other languages an applicant speaks or writes unless the job requires the applicant to speak and/or write a particular language fluently. Rarely is it appropriate to ask an applicant's age, although there are a few exceptions. If required for the job, you may ask if the applicant is over a particular age (for example, a bartender or cocktail server). Be aware that some questions about an applicant's education may be interpreted as seeking information about age. Although it is fine to ask where applicants attended school,

---

4. *Echazabal v. Chevron, USA, Inc.* 2003 U.S. App. Lexis 14670 (9th Cir., 2003)

asking what year they graduated from high school or college, or inquiring if they are "recent graduates," may be deemed discriminatory.

What You Should Do

No single interview style is correct for every circumstance. In some situations, there need only be a single interview and a single interviewer. Where a candidate must be able to work within a team, the interview may be conducted jointly by team members, which can facilitate a "buy-in" on the selection from team members. Take care to avoid overwhelming candidates with too large an interview committee. In the case of executive positions, or other positions requiring interaction with diverse personnel or duties, a series of individual interviews resulting in post-interview reports to the hiring manager may best serve the purpose. In such cases, each participant should have a set of standard interview questions to be asked of each candidate that should, preferably, be pre-approved by the hiring authority.

Selecting Applicants

The number of applications you receive depends on the condition of the job market and the sources you use to find applicants. Often, companies using the Internet to recruit applicants have received hundreds of applications, many of which were inappropriate for the job. The task of weeding through the applications, selecting candidates for interview and conducting interviews can be daunting. Review the following suggestions to facilitate this process.

Screening Applications

When making an initial review of applications, refer to the job specification you developed previously. If you receive only a few applications, it is easy to give them a quick screening to rule out those that do not meet your job specification. If you receive a large number of applications, you may want to use the grid screening technique described below.

Create a grid with the names of the candidates across the top. Then down the side, list the requirements taken from your job specification or job description. Rank each candidate on a scale of 0–5 indicating how strongly they meet each job specification. Base your ranking on evidence contained in their applications.

The grid screening tool organizes and creates a record of your selection process, which you can use to provide evidence of legitimate, job-related criteria (rather than illegal ones, such as race, gender, or age) in making your decisions.

As you review the applications, watch for the following additional issues:

- Give points based only on evidence in the application. Don't make assumptions. It's the applicant's job to tell you what you need to know;

- Be aware of unexplained gaps in employment history or conflicting data;

- Question why an application has minimal or questionable descriptions of responsibilities; and

- If the position requires good communication skills or attention to details, watch for poor grammar or carelessness.

Raise these issues, when applicable, with the candidate if he/she survives the screening process.

Preparing to Interview

Job interviews can be stressful for the candidate and the interviewer. Most people don't do interviews often enough to develop a level of comfort with the task. It's hard to pay attention to a candidate's answer to one question if you're trying to think up the next one. So, it's a good idea to develop, in advance, a written set of core questions that you ask every candidate. By asking all candidates the same core questions, you accomplish the following:

- Give each candidate an equal opportunity to speak to the things you're interested in;

- Obtain the same basic information from all candidates, making it possible for you to compare them; and

- Reduce the legal risk that a candidate could claim differential treatment.

If more than one person is interviewing candidates, be sure each interviewer has the same list of questions. Instruct each interviewer not to deviate from the pre–selected questions.

Schedule interviews so as to give the interviewers enough time to adequately explain the job and elicit information from the candidate. Show the candidate a copy of the job description, preferably before the interview begins, to be sure he/she has an adequate understanding of the job.

Taking Notes

It usually is necessary to take notes during interviews that you can review when later making a final decision about whom to hire. However, it is important to ensure that you are recording interview information in a manner that will not cause you problems in a court of law. Take brief, clear and legible notes that pertain to the candidate's answers only. Don't use abbreviations or a coded rating system that could be misinterpreted at a later date.

Keep objective records of why an applicant was or was not hired to avoid any inference of discriminatory motives. For example:

Table 8. Interview Notetaking

Job or business	Do note	Don't note
Alarm installer	Did not have experience with necessary equipment	Not impressed
Retail clothing store	Unwilling to work weekends	Wasn't right for the job

In addition, be sure that your interview notes evaluate criteria actually necessary to perform the job. For instance, when interviewing for a telemarketer, your notes should reflect items such as "good interpersonal skills, types 75 wpm" rather than "handsome, blue suit."

Telephone Interviews

Preliminary phone interviews can be especially helpful for further screening where you have too many applicants who meet the job qualifications. Phone interviews may also be useful when candidates are located outside of your area and you are not yet ready to provide travel expenses. It's a good idea to schedule phone interviews in advance, so that candidates aren't taken by surprise.

Interviews for Skills and Knowledge

Some interviews are designed to determine the extent of candidates' skills and knowledge. Developing the questions directly from the criteria contained in the job specification or description can help you make the determination. Keep in mind that the questions must be designed to obtain information about the technical skills, education and experience applicable to the essential functions of the job you are seeking to fill.

Example: An interview for a graphic designer might include the following questions:

Example: "The job for which we are recruiting requires frequent design of mail pieces that advertise consumer products for women. Can you tell me about the experience you have designing similar items and how you target them to that audience." or

Example: "Many projects require that the designer also manage the cost for printing and distribution. What education and experience do you have in creating and managing project budgets?"

Behavioral Interviews

Other interviews are designed to reveal how candidates react to situations faced in the job or fit into the culture of an organization. Behavior–based questions may require that candidates tell you how they handled specific situations that are comparable to those they will face on the job at your company. The questions may be designed to draw out information about candidates' attitudes about work, or their strengths and weaknesses. They should, therefore, be designed to draw the candidate out and not to permit one–word or yes–or–no answers. Also avoid questions that elicit "canned answers" such as the typical "...because I want to work with people." Following are examples of behavior–based interview questions.

Example: *We have a lot of long–term servers in our restaurant. When we get busy, they often try to intimidate newer waiters and waitresses to try to get their orders done faster. As a head chef, you need to resolve those situations. Tell us about a similar experience you have had and how you handled it?*

Example: *What specific aspects of your current job duties do you do first and what do you tend to leave to last?* and

Example: *If I asked your co–workers to describe how you work with them, give me examples of what five of them would say.*

Notice that the questions do not ask how the candidate would do something, but rather how he/she has done it in the past. There are often no "right" answers to behavior–based questions. You are seeking predictors of future behavior based on past experience.

Learning About Your Applicants

There is no specific law requiring most employers to check references or backgrounds of prospective employees. However, courts have held employers liable for negligent hiring for certain acts of their employees that the employer should have known might occur.

Example: By initially checking the references of an employee who later assaults someone in your workplace, you could have discovered that the employee had a record of similar assaults. Your actual ignorance of the employee's record is unlikely to be a good defense because with a few simple telephone calls, you could have become aware of the previous assaults. Even if the applicant's former employer refuses to give you any information, documenting that you attempted to check the applicant's prior work history may fulfill your obligation to avoid claims of negligent hiring.

The Law Explained

Both federal and state laws apply to the various kinds of tests and investigations employers use to identify good employment prospects. Federal and state anti-discrimination laws impact testing by requiring that testing instruments and procedures not adversely impact protected classes. Disability discrimination laws, in particular, place restrictions on certain types of tests, including physical examinations and substance abuse screenings and when they can be administered. Other laws protecting privacy rights affect how employers may inquire into the personal and financial history of applicants.

What You Should Do

The following sections guide you through the steps you can take to get to know your applicant in a lawful manner. For a more complete discussion of the law, see the California Chamber's *2004 California Labor Law Digest*.

Medical Examinations

Untimely or unnecessary inquiries about health issues or disabilities leave you in a vulnerable position if you later take adverse action against the applicant or employee. You may require an employee to undergo a physical examination, at your expense, before beginning employment, but only after a conditional job offer has been made. The examination must be job–related and consistent with business necessity and you must require that all entering employees in the same job classification be subject to the same examination.

You may not require an employee or applicant to pay, either directly or by salary deduction, for the cost of any physical examination required as a condition of employment, or required by any law or regulation of federal, state or local government. If you require an employee to have a driver's license as a condition of employment, you must pay the cost of any physical exam that may be required for the issuance of the driver's license, unless the physical exam was completed prior to the time the employee applied for the job.

The following tests are not considered medical examinations:

- Tests to determine the current use of illegal drugs;

- Physical agility tests, which measure an employee's ability to perform actual or simulated job tasks and physical fitness tests, which measure an employee's performance of physical tasks, such as running or lifting — as long as these tests are job related and do not include examinations that could be considered medical (e.g., measuring heart rate or blood pressure);

- Tests that evaluate an employee's ability to read labels or distinguish objects as part of a demonstration of the ability to perform actual job functions;

- Psychological tests that measure personality traits, such as honesty, preferences and habits; and

- Polygraph examinations — although severely limited by state and federal law.

It is illegal for an employer subject to the California FEHA to test an employee or applicant for the presence of a genetic characteristic.

Polygraph Tests

You may not use polygraph (lie detector) tests as pre-employment screening devices. Suggesting that applicants undergo such tests or rejecting an applicant for refusing to take a lie detector test is a violation of federal law.[5] California employers are similarly restricted by state law.[6] However, there are limited exceptions for certain security personnel and employees working with controlled substances. Check with legal counsel if you contemplate hiring candidates in those roles.

Drug Tests

The subject of drug testing in employment is a complex one. This book limits its discussion to some important considerations regarding drug testing during the hiring process. Any drug testing program should be implemented with the advice of legal counsel to ensure compliance with state and federal laws.

Drug testing is not required by law for most employers. One important exception is mandatory drug testing for certain transportation employees under the Omnibus Transportation Employee Testing Act (OTETA).

---

5. 29 U.S.C. 2001–2009
6. Labor Code Section 432.2

More information about the OTETA can be found in the California Chamber's *2004 California Labor Law Digest*. Another exception is for employers with state or federal contracts requiring drug–free workplace programs.

Unless drug testing is required by law or contract, you must decide whether to implement a drug testing program for your applicants. Drug testing always raises questions about an individual's right to privacy, guaranteed under California's constitution, versus an employer's right and obligation to create a safe workplace. Drug testing for applicants generally has become an accepted practice required by many employers as a condition of hiring. If you require drug testing of applicants, have the applicants sign a release before the testing procedure. No sample release is provided with this book, as the release should be specific to the type of testing performed in each employment setting. A competent testing facility should provide you with a release to be signed by each applicant who will undergo a drug test. Decide whether testing will be done for all positions, or only those with potential safety concerns. Once you've determined which positions will require drug testing, be consistent about testing all applicants being considered for those positions.

Of course, drug tests need not be performed on every individual who submits an application for employment, but rather only on those who reach a predetermined stage of the hiring process.

Be consistent. All offers of employment for positions that require drug testing should be made conditional on passing the drug screen.

If you require drug testing as part of a physical exam, keep in mind that both ADA and California law allow a physical exam *only* after a conditional offer of employment is made. Therefore, do not conduct drug testing in conjunction with any *pre-*employment physical examination.

Be certain that the applicant has successfully passed the drug screen before you put him/her to work. Because testing of current employees is severely limited in California, the last thing you want is a brand–new employee whose drug screen comes back positive. For more information about drug testing, see the California Chamber's *2004 California Labor Law Digest*.

Psychological Tests

If you choose to use psychological testing, select a well–accepted test from a reputable testing organization that is designed to identify personality traits related to the job being filled. Care must be taken in the use of psychological testing of applicants. Testing must be job–related and validated as such. Tests must also be shown to treat members of protected classes equally. In California, you must justify psychological testing by a compelling interest in light of the state's constitutional right to privacy. For example, you cannot justify including in a psychological test some questions about religious beliefs and sexual orientation, as there is no relation between those questions and job performance.

Some psychological tests are designed to reveal mental or emotional conditions and are typically administered by a clinical professional. Tests such as these may be considered medical tests, which can only be administered after you make a conditional employment offer.

Written Character Tests

Written "honesty" tests are screening devices used to identify job applicants with propensities to steal money or property on the job. These tests generally avoid privacy concerns because their questions relate more directly to an individual's values, actions and attitudes toward honesty. The key is using a tool from a reputable source and administering it uniformly and fairly. If a written test is administered to a candidate with a disability who is applying for a job for which he or she is otherwise qualified, accommodation must be provided to permit the candidate to take the test.

Skill Tests

Skill tests are tests in which the candidate is asked to perform a task that is representative of an essential job function. For example, a keyboarding test for a data entry position or a written math test for an accounting position. These test must be job related and administered uniformly and fairly. If the essential function is one that a disabled candidate could perform with a reasonable accommodation, such accommodation must be allowed during the test.

Reference Checks

If you intend to check applicants' references, require them to sign a waiver allowing you to investigate all information submitted on the job application. A basic waiver that authorizes you to check past employment, personal references and education is included as part of the sample *Employment Application - Long Form* and sample *Employment Application - Short Form* on the CD that comes with this product.

Review the sample *Reference Check for Employment* on the CD that comes with this product for general questions to ask when checking an applicant's references. When contacting references, the key to obtaining relevant information about an applicant without creating liability for invasion of privacy, is to ask questions related directly to job performance. Use the sample *Guide for Pre-Employment Inquiries* on the CD that comes with this product to determine whether a specific question is acceptable for reference checking. For example, inquiring about the applicant's past attendance record is fine, but a question about the type of illness that kept the employee on sick leave for three weeks is not. Personal references generally are not helpful in the reference checking process as they often are close friends of the applicant and are likely to give a biased report. Improve your chances of obtaining relevant information by requesting personal references who have knowledge of the applicant's work performance, individuals such as past supervisors, subordinates, or clients.

Background Checks

Special rules apply to employers who conduct their own applicant background checks rather than using an outside resource. If you receive information from public records, such as records of arrest, indictment, conviction, civil judicial action, tax lien, or outstanding judgments, you must provide the applicant with a copy of the public record, unless the individual waives the right, in writing, to receive this information. You must provide the copy within seven days, regardless of whether you received the information in written or oral form. The sample *Employment Application - Long Form* and *Employment Application - Short Form* each contain the required notice of this right to the applicant and a check box by which it can be waived.

If you take any adverse action, including denying employment, as a result of receiving information contained in public records, you must provide the applicant with a copy of the public record even though he/she may have waived rights to receive a copy.

Credit Check

Both state and federal laws place restrictions on the use of credit information obtained from consumer credit reporting agencies in the hiring process. The federal Fair Credit Reporting Act (FCRA) places certain restrictions on an employer's ability to use credit reports for employment purposes. This federal law is more restrictive than the California law is relating to the use of credit reports for employment purposes.

Under the federal FCRA, complete the following four steps whenever information from a credit report is used for employment purposes:

1. **Written Disclosure** — Before the report is obtained, make a clear and conspicuous written disclosure to the applicant or employee, in a document consisting solely of the disclosure, that a consumer report may be obtained. See the sample *Notice of Intent to Obtain Consumer Report* on the CD that comes with this product.

2. **Written Authorization** — Obtain prior written authorization from the applicant or employee, using the sample *Authorization to Obtain Consumer Credit Report* on the CD that comes with this product.

3. **Certification to Consumer Reporting Agency** — Use the sample *Certification to Consumer Credit Reporting Agency* on the CD that comes with this product to certify to the consumer reporting agency that the:

   - Disclosure has been made;

   - Authorization has been obtained; and

   - Information will not be used in violation of any federal or state equal opportunity law or regulation.

   You also must certify that if any adverse action is taken based on the consumer report, you will give the applicant or employee a copy of the report and the *Summary of Your Rights Under the Fair Credit Reporting Act* notice, which is on the CD that comes with this product.

4. **Adverse Action Notice** — If any adverse action is taken that is based, at least in part, on information contained in a consumer report, you are required to notify the applicant or employee. See the sample *Adverse Action Notice* on the CD that comes with this product for an example of a written form you can use. The notification may be done in writing, orally, or by electronic means and must include the following:

   - Name, address and telephone number of the consumer reporting agency (including a toll–free telephone number, if it is a nationwide consumer reporting agency) that provided the report;

   - A statement that the consumer reporting agency did not make the adverse decision and is not able to explain why the decision was made;

   - A statement setting forth the applicant's or employee's right to obtain a free disclosure of his or her files from the consumer reporting agency if he or she requests the report within 60 days; and

   - A statement setting forth the applicant's or employee's right to dispute directly with the consumer reporting agency the accuracy or completeness of any information provided by the consumer reporting agency.

   In addition to the requirements under the FCRA, California law requires you to provide a statement to the applicant or employee that the decision to take adverse action was based, in whole or part, upon the information contained in the consumer credit report.

   You are restricted from providing credit information to an employee's creditors who may contact the you, unless the employee has expressly authorized the disclosure in a written release. An employer may not discriminate against an employee or job applicant solely because the individual has filed for bankruptcy.

Investigative Consumer Reports

An investigative consumer report is an in depth report about an applicant that includes:

- Criminal and civil records;

- Driving records;

- Civil lawsuits;

- Reference checks; and

- Any other information obtained by a consumer reporting agency.

Your failure to complete any of the following steps can result in fines, damage claims, punitive damage claims and litigation expenses:

1. You must certify to the consumer reporting agency that you will obey the requirements and limitation of the Fair Credit Reporting Act. The certification must state that:

    - An investigative consumer report will be made regarding the applicant's or employee's character, general reputation, personal characteristics and mode of living;

    - The permissible purpose of the report is to evaluate the applicant or employee for initial or continued employment;

    - You will use the information for employment purposes only and not for any purpose that would violate federal or state equal opportunity law;

    - You will obtain all the necessary disclosures and consents from the subject of the report; and

    - You will give the required notices in the event that an adverse action is taken against an applicant based, in whole or in part, on the contents of the report.

    Use the sample *Certification to Investigative Consumer Reporting Agency* on the CD that comes with this product to complete this step.

2. You must obtain a written release and disclosure signed by the applicant before obtaining the investigative consumer report. A special form is required in California because of state law requiring specific language and a check box with which to obtain a copy of the report. You may use the sample *Disclosure and Authorization to Obtain Investigative Consumer Report* on the CD that comes with this product.

If the applicant makes a written request for a copy of the report, you have five days from receipt of the report to respond and provide a required copy of the Federal Trade

Commission (FTC) publication, *Summary of Your Rights Under the Fair Credit Reporting Act*, a sample of which is on the CD that comes with this product.

3. If adverse action is intended, in full or in part, as a result of the report, then the applicant is entitled to receive the following documents before you take the adverse action:

- A copy of the report;
- A *Summary of Your Rights Under the Fair Credit Reporting Act*; and
- A *Pre-Adverse Action Disclosure,* a sample of which is on the CD that comes with this product.

This information gives the applicant the opportunity to contact the investigative consumer reporting agency to dispute or explain what is in the report. This step also serves your interest by giving an applicant the chance to respond to adverse information before you reject the application for an incorrect reason and waste the time and money you have spent on the recruiting process. If the applicant contests something in the report, you may decide to give him or her a reasonable time to clear the matter and then order a new report, going through the steps a second time.

4. If, after sending out the *Pre-Adverse Action Disclosure* discussed in Step 3, you decide to make the adverse decision final, you must send the applicant an *Adverse Action Notice* advising that you made a final decision, along with another copy of the FTC's *Summary of Your Rights Under the Fair Credit Reporting Act*. A sample *Adverse Action Notice* is on the CD that comes with this product.

Records Retention

It is prudent to keep credit and investigative consumer reports in a private file, apart from an employee's personnel file. As with all private financial and medical records, restrict access to credit and investigative consumer reports to those with a need to know for legitimate business purposes. For example, an executive assistant reviewing a personnel file for year–end attendance records has no need to know that employee's credit card balances or payment history.

Similarly, keep all health and medical information in a separate health file and make it available only to those individuals who need to know the information for the purposes of administering health benefits, leaves of absence or workers' compensation.

Determining Starting Pay

You must keep in mind both legal and practical issues when setting the initial pay rate for a new employee. Legal considerations include compliance with federal and state minimum wage and overtime laws, equal pay laws and avoiding claims of unlawful discrimination. Practical considerations include knowing what it takes to attract the candidate, how the proposed pay rate fits in to your compensation structure and, of course, what you can afford to pay.

The Law Explained

Federal and state minimum wage laws set the base for determining what you must pay a new employee. Because California's minimum wage is higher than the federal minimum, you must comply with the California rate. For employees who are not exempt from overtime, you must also comply with the more generous of federal or state overtime rules, which will, in most cases, be those contained in the California Industrial Wage Order applicable to your business. For more information, see "Determining Exempt or Non-Exempt Status" on page 84.

Some special rules permitting the payment of subminimum wages to certain minors are covered in "Employing Minors" in Chapter 2, page 15.

Equal Pay Laws

Equal pay laws exist at both the federal and state level. Although these laws do not dictate what you must pay to a particular job, they do require that men and women receive equal compensation for equal work on jobs that:

- Require equal skill, effort and responsibility;

- Are performed under similar working conditions—except where you can show that such payment is made pursuant to a:

  - Seniority system;

  - Merit system;

  - System measuring earnings by quantity or quality of production; or

- Are justified by a differential based on any other factor other than sex.[7]

The equal work standard does not require that compared jobs be identical, only that they be substantially equal. The rate of pay must be equal for persons performing equal

---

7. 29 U.S.C. 206(d)

work on jobs requiring equal skill, effort and responsibility and performed under similar working conditions. When factors such as seniority, education, or experience are used to determine the rate of pay, then those standards must be applied on a sex neutral basis. Application of the equal pay standard is not dependent on job classifications or titles, but depends rather on actual job requirements and performance.

Where an employee of one sex is hired or assigned to a particular job to replace an employee of the opposite sex but receives a lower rate of pay than the person replaced, a prima facie violation of the EPA exists. When a prima facie violation of the EPA exists, it is incumbent on the employer to show that the wage differential is justified under one or more of the Act's four affirmative defenses.

 Prima facie (from the Latin meaning "on its face") refers to a situation where a fact *appears* obvious and the party seeking to disprove it must present opposing evidence.

If a person of one sex succeeds a person of the opposite sex on a job at a higher rate of pay than the predecessor and there is no reason for the higher rate other than difference in gender, a violation as to the predecessor is established and that person is entitled to recover the difference between his/her pay and the higher rate paid the successor employee. For more information, see the EEOC's regulations on the Equal Pay Act at ***http://www.access.gpo.gov/nara/cfr/waisidx_03/29cfr1620_03.html***.

New for 2004 The California Court of Appeal recently addressed the issue of whether an employee proved her claim under California's equal pay law.[8] Paula Green worked as a construction superintendent for Par Pools, Inc. At one point during her employment, Par hired a male construction superintendent and paid him more than Green. After being terminated, Green claimed that Par had violated the Equal Pay Act. The trial court ruled in Par's favor and Green appealed.

The appeals court said that, in order to prove an equal pay violation, an employee must first show that the employer paid workers of one sex more than workers of the opposite sex for equal work. The employee need not show that the employer intentionally discriminated against the employee. Green met this requirement by showing that a male construction supervisor was paid more than she was for identical work.

The burden then shifted to Par to show that one of the defenses applied. Par relied on the "catch–all" exception, which allows employers to differentiate in pay for "any bona fide factor other than sex." Such factors include superior experience, education and ability, if the distinction is not based on gender. Par proved that the male construction supervisor had 21 years of experience as a swimming pool construction superintendent and was able to immediately begin supervising 50 projects without a probationary period. Green, on the other hand, had been out of the swimming pool

---

8. Labor Code section 1197.5

industry for two years at the time she was employed and needed a probationary period for training. Her prior experience was primarily administrative office experience.

Green was unable to rebut Par's evidence with a showing that the stated reasons were pretext. Therefore, her equal pay claim failed.[9]

Of similar concern is the avoidance of discrimination claims based on a pattern of compensation differentials between members of different protected classes that cannot be justified. Thus, where an analysis of an employer's payroll shows that members of one racial or ethnic group are generally paid at a lower rate than another doing jobs of similar skill, effort and responsibility, the burden shifts to the employer to show some lawful justification.

Finally, you must be aware of the relative wages of older and younger workers. It sometimes happens, particularly in a competitive job market, that compensation that must be paid to attract a new employee may be close to or even exceed that of long-term, older employees. This results in both poor employee morale and legal exposure to age discrimination claims.

What You Should Do

A full discussion of compensation practices is beyond the scope of this book, but following is some advice you should consider.

First, keeping accurate and up-to-date job descriptions makes it easier to compare the skill, effort and responsibility of jobs when addressing equal pay issues. Current job descriptions also facilitate surveying the community to determine what similar jobs are being paid. This information is critical to keep you competitive not only in hiring, but also in retaining current employees.

Second, periodically review the compensation of employees sharing the same or similar jobs to be sure the earnings of your experienced employees stay above the starting rate at which you must hire. This "wage compression" can be bad for morale and result in the loss of valuable employees.

Finally, stay up-to-date on local area wages, salaries and benefits paid to jobs similar to those in your company. Formal and informal wage and benefit surveys of businesses, conducted by private organizations, industry and trade associations, chambers of commerce and government agencies can help you do this. Some employers have even been known to telephone their competitors posing as a job applicant to obtain wage ranges for competitive jobs. Members of the California Chamber can access wage survey information at ***http://www.hrcalifornia.com/salaries_recruiting/***.

---

9. *Green v. Par Pools, Inc.*, 111 Cal. App. 4th 620 (2003)

Determining Exempt or Non–Exempt Status

It is a good idea to state, prior to the start of employment, whether an employee will be exempt or non–exempt for purposes of wage and hour laws. If the employee will be exempt, phrase the pay rate in weekly, biweekly, or monthly terms of dollars. If the employee will be non–exempt, phrase the pay rate in terms of dollars per hour, because non–exempt employees must be paid overtime based on their hourly rates.

The Law Explained

Federal and state laws exempt certain employees from wage and hour requirements. If you have a problem distinguishing between exempt and non–exempt personnel in your company, you are not alone. An exempt employee normally is an executive, administrative, or professional employee. Other types of exempt employees are those considered to be learned or artistic professionals, outside salespeople, or certain computer–related professionals. All others are non–exempt employees.

The distinction between exempt and non–exempt employees is not always a clear one. Generally, exempt employees are your key personnel who have management and decision–making responsibilities. Because of the complexity of this area of the law and the potential for fines and awards of back overtime pay when an employee is misclassified, this book contains an extensive discussion of the subject and sample worksheets to assist you.

All non–exempt employees are subject to the wage and hour laws of the state or federal government, depending upon which law is more beneficial to the employee. To avoid the payment of overtime premiums, an employee must be exempt from the overtime requirements of both state and federal law.

Merely placing an employee on a salary does not exempt that employee from wage and hour laws. A non–exempt employee placed on a "salary" earns overtime the same as an hourly wage earner does. Further, misclassifying an employee can be a costly mistake.

 If you are not experienced in determining exempt/non–exempt statuses, or are unsure about the status of a particular position, have competent labor legal counsel review your determination.

Similarly, titles are irrelevant to the determination of whether an employee is exempt or non–exempt. Employees with impressive titles may not qualify as exempt if their actual duties do not qualify for an exemption. For example, an employee who performs routine bookkeeping tasks does not become an exempt employee by being given the title of "controller" rather than "bookkeeper."

Federal Law

The Fair Labor Standards Act (FLSA), initially enacted in 1938, sets the minimum wage for the United States and regulates overtime and child labor. All workers employed in interstate commerce are covered by the FLSA. The definition of interstate commerce is broad and most employees are covered. Non–exempt employees are those who are covered by the FLSA and are entitled to overtime. Exempt employees are those who are not covered by the FLSA and are not entitled to overtime. The FLSA is administered and enforced by the Wage and Hour Division of the U.S. Department of Labor (DOL). The federal regulations concerning exempt employees generally are found in Title 29, Part 541 of the Code of Federal Regulations. The FLSA does not automatically preempt any state law regarding overtime and exempt/non–exempt status of employees. The law that is best for the employee will govern.

Federal "white collar" exemptions from overtime law generally are found in Title 29, Part 541 of the Code of Federal Regulations. You can view these regulations on the DOL's website at ***http://www.dol.gov/dol/allcfr/esa/title_29/part_541/toc.htm***. Other common exemptions under federal law are explained on the same website at ***http://www.elaws.dol.gov/flsa/screen75.asp***.

California Law

In California, employees are governed by 17 Industrial Welfare Commission (IWC) Wage Orders. Wage and overtime laws are enforced by the Division of Labor Standards Enforcement (DLSE), through the Labor Commissioner's office.

If your business is covered by an industry order, the industry order applies to all classifications of employees, regardless of what type of work they do for you. You can print Wage Orders on the California Chamber's website, ***HR California***, at ***http://www.hrcalifornia.com***. The following table lists the industry wage orders:

Table 9. Wage Orders

Order number	Industry or Description
Order 1–2001	Manufacturing Industry
Order 2–2001	Personal Service Industry
Order 3–2001	Canning, Freezing and Preserving Industry
Order 5–2001	Public Housekeeping Industry
Order 6–2001	Laundry, Linen Supply, Dry Cleaning and Dyeing Industry
Order 7–2001	Mercantile Industry
Order 8–2001	Industries Handling Products After Harvest

Table 9. Wage Orders

Order number	Industry or Description
Order 9–2004	Transportation Industry
Order 10–2001	Amusement and Recreation Industry
Order 11–2001	Broadcasting Industry
Order 12–2001	Motion Picture Industry
Order 13–2001	Industries Preparing Agricultural Products For Market, on the Farm
Order 16–2001	On–site Construction, Drilling, Logging and Mining Industries
Order 17–2001	Miscellaneous Employees

If a business is not covered by an industry wage order, its employees normally are covered by an occupation order. The Occupation Orders are:

Table 10. Occupation Orders

Order number	Occupation
Order 4–2001	Professional, Technical, Clerical, Mechanical and Similar Occupations
Order 14–2001	Agricultural Occupations
Order 15–2001	Household Occupations

Most employees who are not covered by industry orders are covered by Order 4, based on their occupations. Any employee not covered by a specific Wage Order is covered by Order 17.

Under California law, employees may be exempt from the overtime provisions of the 17 Wage Orders if they are employed in administrative, executive, or professional capacities. These exemptions require that the employee is:

- Engaged in work that is primarily intellectual, managerial, or creative and that:

  - It requires the exercise of discretion and independent judgment; and

  - The remuneration is paid as a salary and is not less than the minimum salary level discussed in "Salary Test for Exempt Employees" on page 87; or

- Licensed or certified by the state of California and is engaged in the practice of one of the following recognized professions:

  - Law;

– Medicine;

– Dentistry;

– Optometry;

– Architecture;

– Engineering;

– Teaching;

– Accounting; or

– Is engaged in an occupation commonly recognized as a learned or artistic profession (Wage Orders 1, 4, 5, 9 and 10 only).

Classifying Other Professions

Registered nurses are not considered to be exempt professional employees unless they individually meet the administrative, executive, or professional criteria described in this section. However, under California law, certified nurse midwives, certified nurse anesthetists and certified nurse practitioners may be exempted from overtime if they are primarily engaged in performing duties for which state certification is required. These employees must still meet the other requirements established for executive, administrative and professional employee exemptions (the salary test and use of discretion and independent judgment).

Participants in national service programs, such as Americorps, are exempted from state employment laws relating to wages, hours and working conditions. Non-profit organizations and other entities using the services of Americorps volunteers must inform participants of any overtime requirements prior to the beginning of service and offer participants the chance to opt out of the program. Participants may not be discriminated against or be denied continued participation in a program for refusing to work overtime for a legitimate reason. The exemptions appear in all 17 Wage Orders, but Order 5 contains special language related to the nursing profession.

Salary Test for Exempt Employees

Exempt employees must be paid at least a minimum level of compensation in the form of a salary, also known as "remuneration." California employers must follow both state and federal regulations regarding an exempt employee's salary. Doing so can be difficult because the state and federal regulations overlap and sometimes are inconsistent with each other. Following are some of the important issues that you, as a California employer, should know about exempt employee salaries.

Minimum Salary

The minimum salary level for California-based exempt white collar employees is "no less than two times the state minimum wage for full time employment." "White collar" exemptions refer to the executive, administrative and professional exemptions discussed throughout this chapter.

The minimum salary level for exempt employees is $2,340 a month. This amount is arrived at by multiplying the state minimum wage by 2,080 hours, multiplying by two and dividing by 12 months ($6.75 x 2,080 = $14,040 x 2 = $28,080/12 = $2,340). Salary is limited to cash wages. It may not include payments "in kind," such as the value of meals and lodging.

Special minimums apply to certain doctors who are paid hourly (see ""Exemption for Physicians/Surgeons Paid Hourly" on page 100) and computer professionals (see "Computer Professional Exemption" on page 101).

Salary Basis

Each pay period, exempt employees must receive a predetermined amount, constituting all or part of their compensation, on a weekly (or less frequent) basis. The amount cannot be subject to reduction because of variations in the quality or quantity of the work performed.

As a general rule, exempt employees need not be paid for any workweek in which they perform no work. Subject to certain exceptions, the employees must receive their full salaries for any week in which they perform any work without regard to the number of days or hours worked.

You may not make deductions from an employee's predetermined compensation for absences required by you or by the operating requirements of your business. Accordingly, if the employee is ready, willing and able to work, deductions may not be made for time when work is not available. However, you are not required to pay an employee's salary for a workweek in which an employee performs no work.

While compensating an employee based on hours worked defeats the salary test required for exempt employees, an employer may pay an exempt employee for hours in excess of the standard 40 workweek, in addition to the employee's regular salary. If the standard workweek in a particular industry is fewer than 40 hours, the Labor Commissioner allows an hourly rate for all hours beyond the industry standard. In addition, any hourly rate paid to otherwise exempt employees for work in excess of eight hours in any one day will not affect the exempt employee's status.

Salary (remuneration) is limited to cash wages. It may not include payments in kind, such as the value of meals and lodging. The salary test can be met on either a monthly or weekly basis. In other words, the salary test is met if the employee is paid at least the minimum amount required once each month, or the employee may be paid weekly with at least the minimum monthly amount multiplied by 12 and divided by 52.

 Employees who are in training for exempt positions are not exempt unless they actually perform the duties of the exempt positions.

Permissible Salary Deductions

Deductions from the predetermined salary may be imposed when employees are absent from work for a day or more for personal reasons other than sickness or accident. Deductions also may be made for absences of one day or more due to sickness or disability if the deduction is made in accordance with a bona fide plan, policy, or practice of providing compensation for loss of salary due to sickness and disability. If your particular plan, policy, or practice provides compensation for such absences, deductions for absences of a day or longer because of sickness or disability may be made before employees have qualified under the plan, policy, or practice and after they have exhausted their leave allowance. It is not required that the employees be paid any portion of their salary for days on which they receive compensation for leave under such plan, policy or practice.

Similarly, employers operating under state sickness and disability insurance law or a private sickness and disability insurance plan, can make deductions for absences of one work day or longer — if benefits are provided in accordance with the particular law or plan. In the case of an industrial accident, the "salary basis" requirement is met if the employee is compensated for loss of salary in accordance with the workers' compensation law or the plan adopted by the employer, provided the employer also has some plan, policy or practice of providing compensation for sickness and disability other than that relating to industrial accidents.

An employee's salary may be prorated in full day increments for the initial and final weeks of work. However, this should not be construed to mean that employees are on a salary basis within the meaning of the regulations if they are employed occasionally for a few days and are paid a proportionate part of the weekly salary when so employed. Moreover, even payment of the full weekly salary under such circumstances would not meet the requirement, because casual or occasional employment for a few days at a time is inconsistent with employment on a salary basis

Leave taken under the federal FMLA and California Family Rights Act (CFRA) by an exempt employee will not affect the exempt status of the employee. Thus, employers may make deductions from the exempt employee's salary and/or benefits (such as paid sick leave) for hours taken as intermittent or reduced FMLA/CFRA leave, without affecting the exempt status of the employee.

Forbidden Salary Deductions

Although federal regulation and court decisions allow deductions from an exempt employee's salary in limited circumstances for disciplinary reasons, the state Labor Commissioner recently stated in a legal opinion that "the federal regulations which purport to allow deductions for infractions of any rule are not compatible with California law and will not be allowed."

New for 2004 Deductions from an exempt employee's salary may be made for absences caused by jury duty, attendance as a witness, or temporary military leave if the employee has performed no work within the workweek.[10] The employer may also offset any amounts received by an employee as jury or witness fees or military pay for a particular week against the salary due for that particular week without loss of the exemption.

State pregnancy disability leave regulations allow an employer to require an employee to use available, accrued sick leave for partial day absences. The same regulations specify that an employee may elect, at her option, to use any vacation time or other accrued time off for partial day absences. However, unlike the federal family leave regulations, the pregnancy disability leave regulations do not address whether making such partial day deductions from salary (even when replaced by sick/vacation pay) affects exempt status. Therefore, employers considering making partial day deductions for exempt employees disabled by pregnancy would be wise to consult with legal counsel.

What You Should Do

You are not required by law to fill out and/or save exemption worksheets to determine whether an employee should be classified as exempt or non-exempt. However, the worksheets are an excellent way to define an employee's job duties and compare them to the various criteria that must be met in order for an employee to be classified properly as exempt or non-exempt. Misclassification of a non-exempt employee as exempt could result in huge awards of back overtime payments plus fines and legal expenses.

Review the sample exemption worksheets on the CD that comes with this product to help determine whether the position you're filling should be classified as exempt or non-exempt. When determining if an employee's duties meet the requirements for an exemption, keep in mind that an employee who does not perform exempt duties on a regular basis cannot be classified as exempt for a temporary assignment unless he/she:

---

10. DLSE Enforcement Manual (2002) Section 51.6.21.1

- Works the exempt job for at least one month; and

- Meets the duties and salary tests. For more information, see "Salary Test for Exempt Employees" on page 87.

 There is an exception for the motion picture industry. Wage Order 12 allows a short–term "equivalent" to the monthly amount. Under this wage order, an exempt employee may be paid for a period as short as one week if the amount is proportionate to the required monthly minimum ($2,340 x 12 = $28,080/52 = $540).

You usually complete the worksheet based on the job description for the position. However, consider involving the employees who are filling the position in completing the worksheets. They can assist in determining the exact duties performed on a regular basis and the amount of time employees actually spend on various tasks, as this may differ greatly from time allocated for those tasks in a written job description. Keep completed exempt analysis worksheets in the employee's personnel file, or with other worksheets in a common file. You can use them for reference when hiring for similar positions in the future.

You may also use the worksheets periodically to reconsider the status of existing positions if the job content changes or when the amount of time spent on exempt versus non–exempt duties changes. The following sections discuss issues relating to particular exemptions.

Executive Exemption

An executive is one who is in charge of a unit with permanent status and function and who ordinarily supervises the activities of others. To be exempt as an executive, an employee must meet all of the following tests:

- The primary duty must be the management of the enterprise, or of a customarily recognized department or subdivision;

- The employee must customarily and regularly direct the work of at least two or more other employees;

- The employee must have the authority to hire and fire, or to command particularly serious attention to his or her recommendations on such actions affecting employees; and

- The employee must customarily and regularly exercise discretionary power;

In 2000, the IWC expanded the way it construes the definition of "primarily engaged in exempt work" so that it now includes "all work that is directly and closely related to exempt work and work which is properly viewed as a means for carrying out exempt functions." This means that exempt employees must spend more than 50% of their time performing:

- Exempt duties;

- Work that is directly and closely related to exempt work; or

- Work that is properly viewed as a means for carrying out exempt functions.

The employee must meet the salary test discussed in "Salary Test for Exempt Employees" on page 87.

 For more information, review the sample *Exempt Analysis Worksheet - Executive/Managerial Exemption* and sample *Job Description - Managerial or Executive Exemption* on the CD that comes with this product.

Managerial Duties: Exempt vs. Non-exempt

Exempt duties under the Executive Exemption must be directly and clearly related to the managerial work. Exempt duties include:

- Interviewing, selecting and training employees;

- Setting and adjusting pay rates and work hours or recommending same;

- Directing work;

- Keeping production records of subordinates for use in supervision;

- Evaluating employees' efficiency and productivity;

- Handling employees' complaints;

- Disciplining employees;

- Planning work;

- Determining work;

- Distributing work;

- Deciding on types of merchandise, materials, supplies, machinery, or tools; and

- Controlling flow and distribution of merchandise, materials and supplies.

In comparison, examples of non–exempt duties under the Executive Exemption include:

- Performing the same kind of work as subordinates;

- Performing any production work, even though not like that performed by subordinate employees, which is not part of a supervisory function;

- Making sales, replenishing stock and returning stock to shelves, except for supervisory training or demonstration;

- Performing routine clerical duties, such as bookkeeping, cashiering, billing, filing, or operating business machines;

- Checking and inspecting goods as a production operation, rather than as a supervisory function; and

- Performing maintenance work.

Supervisors

If an employee is supervising only two or three other office employees, the main responsibilities and duties of the supervising employee are often directed toward performing office functions. Although these office functions may require more skill than those performed by the subordinates, they nevertheless may be routine office work or bookkeeping that is non–exempt work.

Working Managers

A working manager is exempt only if his/her managerial duties constitute more than half of the work time and the employee receives little or no supervision in day–to–day operations.

Examples of industries employing working managers who usually are non–exempt include:

- Service stations;

- Restaurants;

- Rest homes;

- Branch retail stores; and

- Motels.

A working manager cannot be exempt if he/she is engaged primarily in activities such as cooking, selling on the floor, cashiering, pumping gas, keeping records, taking care of patients, or acting as a desk clerk. Assistants to managers and trainees usually are non-exempt. They do not customarily and regularly direct the work of other employees, but rather share the responsibility, or are learning the position and not performing the duties of the exempt position on a regular basis.

Managers of apartment houses usually are non-exempt. However, if the facility and staff are large enough, an apartment manager may meet the duties test for an exempt executive.

Administrative Exemption

The exempt administrative employee is one who:

- Customarily and regularly exercises discretion and independent judgment in the performance of intellectual work that, in the context of an administrative function, is office or non-manual work directly related to management policies or the general business operations of you or your customers;

- Regularly and directly assists a proprietor or an exempt administrator; performs, under only general supervision, work along specialized or technical lines requiring special training, experience, or knowledge; or executes special assignments and tasks under only general supervision;

- Devotes more than 50% of his/her work to administrative duties; and

- The employee meets the salary test discussed in "Salary Test for Exempt Employees" on page 87.

 Discretion and independent judgment involve comparing and evaluating possible courses of conduct and acting or making a decision after considering various possibilities. It implies that the employee has the power to make an independent choice free from immediate supervision and with respect to matters of significance. The decision may be in the form of a recommendation for action, subject to the final authority of a superior, but the employee must have sufficient authority for the recommendations to affect matters of consequence to the business or its customers.

Employees who merely apply their knowledge in following prescribed procedures or in determining which procedures to follow, or who determine whether specified standards are met or whether an object falls into one or another grade or class, are not exercising discretion and judgment of the independent sort associated with administrative work. Inspectors and graders, for example, may have some leeway regarding the application of knowledge to a particular situation, but only within closely prescribed limits. Almost every employee must make decisions requiring discretion. The requirement for this exemption is that the decisions must involve matters of consequence that are of real and substantial significance to the policies or general operations of your business or customers. The tasks may be directly related to only a particular segment of the business, but still must have a substantial effect on the whole business.

Exercising discretion and independent judgment on matters of consequence is distinguished from making decisions that can lead to serious loss through the choice of wrong techniques, improper application of skills, neglect, or failure to follow instructions. To "customarily and regularly" exercise discretion and independent judgment is to do so frequently in the course of day–to–day activities. The phrase signifies a frequency that is more than occasional, but may be less than constant.

Three types of administrative employees who may qualify for an exemption are:

- Executive or administrative assistants;

- Staff employees who are functional rather than department heads; and

- Employees who perform special assignments under only general supervision.

Executive or Administrative Assistants

Executive or administrative assistants to whom executives or high level administrators have delegated part of their discretionary powers may have enough authority to qualify for the administrative exemption. Generally, such assistants are found in large establishments where executives or administrators have duties that are of such scope and which require so much attention, that the work of personal scrutiny, personal attention to correspondence and conducting personnel interviews must be delegated. Titles are various and unreliable and include:

- Executive secretary;

- Assistant to the general manager;

- Assistant buyer (retail); and

- Vice principal (private schools).

Staff Employees

The category of staff employees includes employees who are functional rather than department heads and employees who act as advisory specialists to management or to your customers. Examples include:

- Tax experts;

- Insurance experts;

- Sales research experts;

- Wage-rate analysts; and

- Foreign exchange consultants and statisticians.

Such experts may or may not be exempt, depending on the extent to which they exercise discretionary powers. Also included in this category are persons in charge of a functional department, which might be a one-person department, such as:

- Credit managers;

- Purchasing agents;

- Buyers;

- Personnel directors;

- Safety directors;

- Labor relations directors; and

- Heads of academic departments and special curriculum advisors in private schools.

Employees Performing Special Assignments

Employees who perform special assignments under only general supervision may qualify for the administrative exemption. These include many employees who work away from your business premises, such as:

- Lease buyers;

- Location managers for motion picture companies; and

- Some field representatives.

Titles often do not reflect duties; the managerial-sounding title of "field representative" for a utility company, for example, actually may be a service person.

Special assignments also may be performed on your business premises by employees such as:

- Organization planners;

- Customers' brokers in stock exchange firms;

- Account executives in advertising firms; or

- Persons responsible for developing and maintaining academic programs.

For more information, review the sample *Exempt Analysis Worksheet - Administrative Exemption* and sample *Job Description - Administrative Exemption* on the CD that comes with this product.

Professional Exemption

California's IWC Wage Orders cover most employees in professional capacities. Order 4 regulates the wages and hours of professional, technical, clerical and mechanical occupations. Thus, the professional exemption of federal law is limited by state law.

Professionals who are exempted from the requirements of the IWC Wage Orders generally are those who are licensed or certified by the state and who actively practice one of the following professions:

- Law;
- Medicine;
- Dentistry;
- Optometry;
- Architecture;
- Engineering;
- Teaching; or
- Accounting.

The following table lists those professionals who are exempt from IWC Wage Orders and those who are not.

Table 11. Wage Order Professional Exemption

Professionals exempt from Wage Orders	Professionals not exempt from Wage Orders
Physicians	Nurses
Attorneys	Paralegals
Certified public accountants	Uncertified accountants
Licensed civil, mechanical and electrical engineers	Unlicensed engineers and junior drafters

There is no minimum remuneration required to qualify for the professional exemption under state law.

The IWC Wage Orders cover the following non-exempt employees:

- Registered nurses;

- Professional therapists;

- Medical technologists;

- Statisticians; and

- Uncertified accountants.

However, certified nurse midwives, certified nurse anesthetists and certified nurse practitioners may be exempted from overtime if they are primarily engaged in performing duties for which state certification is required. These employees must still meet the other requirements established for executive, administrative and professional employee exemptions (the salary test and use of discretion and independent judgment). For more information, see "Salary Test for Exempt Employees" on page 87.

Order 4 covers occupations often considered to be among artistic or learned professions, including:

- Artists;

- Copy writers;

- Editors;

- Librarians;

- Nurses;

- Photographers;

- Social workers;

- Statisticians;

- Teachers (other than state certified); and

- Other related occupations listed as professional.

When persons in these occupations are employed in an industry covered by an industry order, they are covered by that order. For example, a news writer employed by a TV broadcasting organization would be covered by Order 11 (Broadcasting) and a social worker employed by a hospital would be covered by Order 5 (Public Housekeeping).

Except for Orders 1 (Manufacturing), 4 (Professional, Technical, Clerical, Mechanical and Similar Occupations), 5 (Public Housekeeping), 9 (Transportation) and 10 (Amusement and Recreation), there may be rare individuals who are exempt because they are employed in a learned profession other than those listed in Section 1 of the Wage Orders. In order to be exempt under the learned profession exemption, the following requirements must be met:

- The educational requirement for the job is advanced, meaning that the employee must have a degree or certificate requiring at least one year of specialized study in addition to completion of a four–year college course;

- The employee's work is of such a nature that its product cannot be standardized with respect to time and the employee has considerable freedom of choice as to when and how to carry out a task, so that the individual generally has control over his or her hours of work; and

- The work is creative or intellectual more than 50% of the time, it depends on imagination or invention, or is involved in analysis and the drawing of conclusions. This is different from the application of ordinary mental skills and knowledge apart from the exercise of discretion and independent judgment. Examples of professionals who might be exempt on this basis would be certain consulting or research chemists, physicists, biologists, geologists, etc., if their work and working conditions fit the criteria.

If these tests are applied, the salary test also must be met.

In Orders 1, 4, 5, 9 and 10, the professional exemption was broadened to state that no person shall be considered to be employed in an administrative, executive, or professional capacity unless one of the following conditions prevail:

- The employee is engaged in work that is primarily intellectual, managerial, or creative and which requires exercise of discretion and independent judgment and for which the monthly salary is not less than two times the state minimum wage for full time employment (see "Minimum Salary" on page 88); or

- The employee is licensed or certified by the state of California and is engaged in the practice of one of the following recognized professions: law, medicine, dentistry, optometry, architecture, engineering, teaching, or accounting, or is engaged in an occupation commonly recognized as a learned or artistic profession. Registered nurses are not considered to be exempt professional employees unless they individually meet the administrative, executive, or professional criteria described in the Wage Order.

Wage Orders 1, 4, 5, 9 and 10 permit exemptions for some medical professionals if they meet the salary test discussed in "Salary Test for Exempt Employees" on page 87 and the following requirements:

- An Opinion Letter issued by DLSE on August 14, 2002, declared that physician assistants, occupational therapists and physical therapists as a class are typically not eligible for exemption as "professional employees" as they are not required to have advanced degrees. The status of particular positions of this kind must be reviewed on a case by case basis;

- Dental hygienists ordinarily do not qualify under the professional exemption. In usual circumstances, a dental hygienist is a highly technical specialist. A dental hygienist who has completed four academic years of pre-professional and professional study in an accredited university or college recognized by the Commission on Accreditation of Dental and Dental Auxiliary Educational Programs of the American Dental Association is considered to have met the professional exemption. In such cases, the determination of exempt status is made on an individual basis and depends upon whether the hygienist meets all the other tests in the regulation; and

- Pharmacists are not automatically considered exempt professionals. To be exempt, pharmacists must individually pass the administrative or executive exemption tests. If they do not pass the administrative or executive exemption tests, they are non-exempt and are, therefore, entitled to overtime, meal and break periods and all other wage and hour protections contained in the IWC Wage Orders.

Exemption for Physicians/Surgeons Paid Hourly

A licensed physician or surgeon who is compensated on an hourly basis and who is primarily engaged in performing duties for which licensure is required is exempt from overtime if he/she is paid $57.56 or more per hour. The $57.56 rate may be adjusted annually by the DIR based on the California Consumer Price Index (CPI). The adjustment will be made each October 1, to be effective the following January 1. This exemption does not apply to employees in medical internships or resident programs, physician employees covered by collective bargaining agreements, or veterinarians.

Exemption for Artistic Professions

Relatively few individuals qualify for exemption as members of artistic professions in California, because most of those who have sufficient control over the nature of their own work and over their work hours are self-employed. Academic degrees are not required, but a specialized course of study of at least four years is generally one element involved in establishing a professional standing in the fine arts. This element by itself, however, is not enough. Composers or vocal instrumental soloists may be exempted because of their wide-ranging discretionary powers, including control over their working conditions. However, members of an orchestra will not exempted.

Some writers employed in the motion picture or broadcast industries have sufficient discretionary powers to be exempt. However, most do not, even when they work at home, because of time limits, restricting outlines, or other constraints on the creative aspects of their work. For example, a newspaper columnist required to furnish five columns per week only, regardless of subject, time of preparation, etc., could be exempted from Order 4; but reporters, editors and advertising copy writers could not be. Any individual exempted by virtue of the creative and discretionary nature of the work in an artistic profession also must meet the salary test.

For more information, review the sample *Exempt Analysis Worksheet - Professional Exemption* on the CD that comes with this product.

Computer Professional Exemption

The state's computer professional exemption is similar to that available under federal law, which says that computer systems analysts, computer programmers, software engineers, or other similarly skilled workers in the computer software field are eligible for exemption only under federal law as professionals. In California, a professional employee in the computer field is exempt from overtime pay if the employee is primarily engaged in:

- Work that is intellectual or creative;

- Work that requires the exercise of discretion and independent judgment;

- Duties that consist of one or more of the following:

  - The application of systems analysis techniques and procedures, including consulting with users, to determine hardware, software, or system functional specifications;

  - The design, development, documentation, analysis, creation, testing, or modification of computer systems or programs, including prototypes based on and related to, user or system design specifications; or

  - The documentation, testing, creation, or modification of computer programs related to the design of software or hardware for computer operating systems.

  - Highly skilled and proficient in the theoretical and practical application of highly specialized information to computer systems analysis, programming and software engineering; and

  - Paid at least $44.63 per hour (though this amount may be adjusted annually by the state). The corresponding federal exemption requires the employee to be paid a minimum of $27.63 hour. California employees must be paid the higher of the two rates in order to qualify for the exemption.

An employee is *not* exempt as a computer professional if any of the following apply:

- The employee is a trainee or employee in an entry-level position who is learning to become proficient in the theoretical and practical application of highly specialized information to computer systems analysis, programming and software engineering;

- The employee is in a computer-related occupation but has not attained the level of skill and expertise necessary to work independently and without close supervision;

- The employee is engaged in the operation of computers or in the manufacture, repair, or maintenance of computer hardware and related equipment;

- The employee is an engineer, drafter, machinist, or other professional whose work is highly dependent upon or facilitated by the use of computers and computer software programs and who is skilled in computer-aided design software, including CAD/CAM, but who is not in a computer systems analysis or programming occupation;

- The employee is a writer engaged in writing material, including labels, product descriptions, documentation, promotional material, setup and installation instructions and other similar written information, either for print or for onscreen media, or who writes or provides content material intended to be read by customers, subscribers, or visitors to computer-related media such as the World Wide Web or CD-ROMs; or

- The employee is creating imagery for effects used in the motion picture, television, or theatrical industry.

 For more information, review the sample *Exempt Analysis Worksheet - Computer Professional Exemption* on the CD that comes with this product.

Outsides Sales Exemption

With guidance from the California Supreme Court and the California Legislature, the IWC has issued new regulations regarding the outside salesperson exemption. Outside salespersons are exempt from overtime requirements if they:

- Are 18 years of age or older; and

- Spend more than 50% of their working time away from your place of business, selling tangible or intangible items, or obtaining orders or contracts for products, services, or use of facilities.

Outside salespersons are not required to meet the minimum salary requirement that applies to the executive/managerial, administrative and professional exemptions.

Unlike federal law, California law does not allow work performed incidental to and in conjunction with, the employee's own outside sales or solicitations, including incidental deliveries and collections, to be considered exempt work. This distinction is particularly important for route salespeople and others who perform many functions other than sales in an average day, such as delivery, repair and maintenance. In order to be exempt, outside salespeople in California must spend at least 50% of their time performing exempt duties. Work performed incidental to and in conjunction with, the employee's outside sales is not considered exempt work in California and cannot exceed 50% of an employee's working time.

 For more information, review the sample *Exempt Analysis Worksheet - Salesperson Exemption* on the CD that comes with this product.

Commissioned Sales Exemption

Employees working under Wage Orders 4 and 7 are not entitled to overtime under California law if their earnings exceed one–and–one–half times the minimum wage and more than half of the employee's compensation represents commissions. Employees also must meet one of the federal exemptions in order to be exempt from federal overtime requirements.

Making the Employment Offer

Now that you have done your research, you are ready to make the offer of employment. For each position to be filled in your company, make it clearly understood that there is only one person authorized to make an employment offer for that particular position.

The Law Explained

Although not required by law, you can avoid misunderstandings as to the job being offered and the conditions of employment by being clear as to who has the authority to make an offer of employment through the use of employment offer letters. During the hiring process, have interviewers make clear to applicants how you make offers of employment and if you use employment offer letters, that an offer letter is the only way an offer can be communicated. You can use the sample *Employment Letter* on the CD that comes with this product.

Although not required to do so, you may wish to send a letter to applicants who are not hired so they know that they are no longer under consideration. There is no need and it is not advisable, to state a reason for passing them over or describing the qualities of the person selected. A simple letter thanking them for their interest and wishing them well in their future employment is sufficient. Send the original letter is to the unsuccessful applicant. You may either keep a copy of each letter or simply keep a list of the applicants who received the letter. As long as a standard letter is sent to each unsuccessful applicant, a list of names is a sufficient record, which saves both paper and filing space. You can use the sample *Letter to Applicants Not Hired* on the CD that comes with this product as is, or adapt it to suit your company's needs.

What You Should Do

Offer letters should, at a minimum, contain:

- Job title;

- Exempt or non-exempt status;

- Starting salary or wage;

- Work schedule;

- Full-time or part-time classification for benefits;

- Reporting date;

- Any conditions to which the offer is subject, such as:

  - Post-offer medical exam;

  - Post-offer drug test;

  - Reference and/or background check.

- A statement of the at-will basis of employment; and

- A deadline by which you expect an acceptance of the position by way of return of a signed copy of the offer letter.

You may send the sample *Employment Letter* as is, or print it on your company letterhead. Keep a copy of the letter in the employee's personnel file. Use the *Hiring Checklist* on the CD that comes with this product to document that the letter was sent.

Depending on the wording of an employment letter, a court may construe it as a contract. The sample *Employment Letter* contains no contractual language and specifies that it is not a contract. Use caution in modifying this letter to avoid creating a contract.

If the employee will be exempt, phrase the pay rate in weekly, biweekly, or monthly terms of dollars. If the employee will be non-exempt, phrase the pay rate in terms of dollars per hour, because non–exempt employees must be paid overtime based on their hourly rates.

Keep in mind that the distinction between exempt and non–exempt employees is not always clear. This chapter contains an extensive discussion of the subject and sample worksheets to assist you in determining of exempt or non–exempt status. For more information see "Determining Exempt or Non–Exempt Status" on page 84.

If you make a job offer contingent on a medical evaluation, drug test, background check, or the fulfillment of any other condition, be sure to note it clearly in the employment letter. Remember that medical evaluations are allowed only after an offer of employment has been made, so make the offer contingent on passing the medical evaluation, drug test or other stated condition. For more information, see "Medical Examinations" on page 73 and "Drug Tests" on page 74. It is illegal for an employer of five or more employees who is covered by the Fair Employment and Housing Act (FEHA) to subject an employee or applicant to a test for the presence of a genetic characteristic. You can also find more information on drug testing in the California Chamber's **2004 California Labor Law Digest**.

Temporary Employees

You may wish to prepare a separate letter for employees hired on a temporary basis that clearly describes the limited duration of their employment in terms of either a specific time or a specific assignment. Send the letter only to individuals hired as temporary employees directly by your company. It is not necessary for temporary employees hired through a temporary or leasing agency. Inform temporary employees that the assignment is not guaranteed for any particular length of time and that they are not eligible for certain company benefits. Include at–will language in this letter, or your description of the temporary assignment may be misunderstood to be a contract for a specified period of time or until the completion of the assignment.

For a sample, see the *Letter to Temporary Employees* on the CD that comes with this product.

What Forms and Checklists Do I Use to Interview and Select Qualified Employees?

The following table describes forms and checklists associated with interviewing and selecting qualified employees.

You can find these forms on the CD that comes with this product.

Table 12. Required Forms and Checklists

Form/Checklist Name	What do I use it for?	When do I use it?	Who fills it out?	Where does it go?
Adverse Action Notice	To take adverse action (such as not hiring an applicant or terminating an employee) based on a credit report you have obtained	When you know you are taking adverse action based on information in the credit report (See "Background Checks" on page 77)	You fill it out and give it to the employee or applicant	Give to employee. Keep a copy in a private file away from personnel file. Restrict access to the form to a "need to know" basis.
Authorization to Obtain Consumer Credit Report	To obtain a credit report of any type	Before you obtain the report (See "Background Checks" on page 77)	You and the employee or applicant fill out respective sections of the form	Keep in personnel file. Restrict access to the form to a "need to know" basis.
Certification to Consumer Credit Reporting Agency	To obtain a credit report of any type	Before you obtain the report (See "Background Checks" on page 77)	You do	Send form to the agency creating the report. Keep in personnel file. Restrict access to the form to a "need to know" basis.
Certification to Investigative Consumer Reporting Agency	To obtain an investigative consumer report	Before you obtain the report (See "Background Checks" on page 77)	You do	Send form to the agency creating the report. Keep in personnel file. Restrict access to the form to a "need to know" basis.

Table 12. Required Forms and Checklists

Form/Checklist Name	What do I use it for?	When do I use it?	Who fills it out?	Where does it go?
Disclosure and Authorization to Obtain Investigative Consumer Report	To obtain an investigative consumer report	Before you obtain the report (See "Background Checks" on page 77)	You and applicant	Personnel file
Notice of Intent to Obtain Consumer Report	To obtain a credit report of any type	Before you obtain the report (See "Background Checks" on page 77)	You do	Keep in personnel file. Restrict access to the form to a "need to know" basis.
Pre-Adverse Action Disclosure	To take adverse action (such as not hiring an applicant or terminating an employee) based on a credit report you have obtained	After you obtain the report. Must be accompanied by copy of the credit report.	You do	Keep in a private file away from personnel files. Restrict access to the form to a "need to know" basis.
Summary of Your Rights Under the Fair Credit Reporting Act	To obtain a credit report of any type	When you give the employee a copy of the credit report	NA	Give to applicant

Table 13. Recommended Forms and Checklists

Form/Checklist Name	What do I use it for?	When do I use it?	Who fills it out?	Where does it go?
Employment Interview Checklist	Listing which questions to ask applicants during an interview	During the applicant's interview	Interviewer	Keep in the employee's personnel file, if hired. If you don't hire the applicant, keep the paperwork for two years.
Employment Letter	Informing an applicant that he or she has been selected for employment	When the employment decision has been made	You do	Mail to the applicant. Keep a copy in the employee's personnel file.
Exempt Analysis Worksheet - Administrative Exemption	Determining whether an employee's duties meet the requirements for exempt status	During the hiring process	You do	Keep in the employee's personnel file
Exempt Analysis Worksheet - Computer Professional Exemption	Determining whether an employee's duties meet the requirements for exempt status	During the hiring process	You do	Keep in the employee's personnel file
Exempt Analysis Worksheet - Executive/ Managerial Exemption	Determining whether an employee's duties meet the requirements for exempt status	During the hiring process	You do	Keep in the employee's personnel file

Table 13. Recommended Forms and Checklists

Form/Checklist Name	What do I use it for?	When do I use it?	Who fills it out?	Where does it go?
Exempt Analysis Worksheet - Professional Exemption	Determining whether an employee's duties meet the requirements for exempt status	During the hiring process	You do	Keep in the employee's personnel file
Exempt Analysis Worksheet - Salesperson Exemption	Determining whether an employee's duties meet the requirements for exempt status	During the hiring process	You do	Keep in the employee's personnel file
Hiring Checklist	Tracking completion of recommended and required hiring procedures and forms	During the recruiting and hiring process	Manager or other person in charge of hiring employees	Keep in the employee's personnel file
Job Description - Administrative Exemption	To assist in properly classifying position as exempt or non-exempt	When preparing or reviewing a job description	You do	Keep in the employee's personnel file
Job Description - Managerial or Executive Exemption	To assist in properly classifying position as exempt or non-exempt	When preparing or reviewing a job description	You do	Keep in the employee's personnel file
Letter to Applicants Not Hired	Informing an applicant that he or she has not been selected for employment	When the employment decision has been made	You do	Mail to the applicant. Keep a list of the applicants to whom the letter is mailed

Table 13. Recommended Forms and Checklists

Form/Checklist Name	What do I use it for?	When do I use it?	Who fills it out?	Where does it go?
Letter to Temporary Employees	Informing a temporary employee of the limited terms of the employment	When the employment decision has been made	You do	Keep in employee's personnel file
Pre-Hire Checklist	Keeping track of pre-hiring activities	Before you hire	No filling out	With your own hiring procedures
Reference Check for Employment	To obtain information about an applicant from former employers	When considering candidate for employment	You do	Keep in employee's personnel file

Chapter 5

Getting New Employees Started Right

It is important, both for your company and for your new employees, that your employment relationships begin properly. The way you introduce a new employee to your company tells a lot about how well organized you are, your company's behavior and performance expectations and the value you place on training. The legal requirements and forms involved every time you hire a new employee are quite extensive. Yet, complying with the law and following an established procedure at the time of hire is your best opportunity to ensure that all new employees:

- Understand your policies and work rules;

- Are informed of their legal rights and obligations;

- Receive the necessary training to do their jobs safely; and

- Are eligible to work in this country.

New Employee Paperwork

You and your new employees are required to fill out certain legally required forms immediately upon hire. To meet this requirement and avoid penalties for failing to do so, use the *Hiring Checklist* on the CD that comes with this product to ensure that you and your employees complete all necessary forms and tasks. The forms you need in this process also are on the CD that comes with this product. Alternately, you may obtain some of them directly from federal and state government agencies. The followings sections describe the legally required forms that you must provide to new employees and what you should do with them (see "Legally Required Forms" on page 112).

The Law Explained

Completing the steps described in the following "What You Should Do" section fulfills many of your legal obligations for maintaining a safe workplace and can help you avoid fines and penalties from government agencies. Doing so also establishes proper documentation should you have to defend your company against a lawsuit.

What You Should Do

To make the hiring process as easy as possible, use the sample *Hiring Checklist* to complete the following steps:

1. Familiarize yourself with the sample *Hiring Checklist*. Forms that are legally required for all California employers are indicated in bold, while forms legally required only for certain California employers are marked with an asterisk (*). To further determine if/how your company is legally required to use a given form, refer to its discussion later in this section.

2. Before meeting with your new employee, gather together the forms you need and read each one and its accompanying information carefully.

3. As you give forms to your new employee, write the date in the "Date Given" column.

4. As the employee returns the completed forms to you, write the date in the "Date Rec'd" column. When forms, such as informational pamphlets, are not required to be returned to you the "Date Rec'd" column is prefilled with "N/A."

5. If a form must be filed or sent, write the date in the "Date Filed/Sent" column when that action is taken.

6. When the *Hiring Checklist* is completed, file it in the employee's personnel file as a permanent record that you have complied with the law and your own established procedures.

Legally Required Forms

This section discusses the legally required forms that California employers must use in the hiring process and recommended forms that help make the job easier. Each form has its own discussion providing you with a clear and concise explanation of why, when and how to use it and what to do with the form once it is completed.

Tax Documents

Prior to their first pay date, new employees must fill out a federal *W-4 Form - Employee's Withholding Allowance Certificate* to declare the number of withholding allowances being claimed. An employee may submit a new *W–4 Form* at any time to reflect a change in marital status or withholding allowances.

When an employee submits a new *W–4 Form*, keep it with all previous *W–4 Forms* in the employee's personnel file, or, if separately maintained, payroll file. Or, keep a copy in the file if you send the original to your payroll department.

You may obtain more information by contacting the Internal Revenue Service (IRS) Information Hotline at (800) 829–1040. Additional forms and tax information may also be obtained on the IRS website at ***http://www.irs.ustreas.gov***.

 For more information, review the sample federal *W-4 Form - Employee's Withholding Allowance Certificate* on the CD that comes with this product.

Employees are not required to fill out the *California Employee's Withholding Allowance Certificate (Form DE 4)*, but it must be available for employees who choose to use it. Because the federal *W–4 Form* also can be used for California withholdings, *Form DE 4* need be filled out only by employees who claim a different marital filing status, number of regular allowances or different additional dollar amount to be withheld for California personal income tax withholding than for federal income tax withholding. When an employee submits a new form, keep it with all previous *Form DE 4* in the employee's personnel file, or, if separately maintained, payroll file. Or, keep a copy if you send the original to your payroll department.

 The *Form DE 4* does not change federal withholding allowances.

You may obtain more information by contacting your local EDD Tax Information office, listed in your local telephone directory in the State Government section under "Employment Development Department." Additional forms and tax information may also be obtained on EDD's website at ***http://www.edd.ca.gov***.

 For more information, review the sample *California Employee's Withholding Allowance Certificate (Form DE 4)* on the CD that comes with this product.

Immigration Documents

An *I-9 Form* must be filled out for each employee hired after November 6, 1986.
Section 1: The employee, or his/her translator or preparer, must fill out Section 1 at the time of hire. The employee must sign this section personally.

Section 2: You must complete Section 2 and examine evidence of identity and employment eligibility within three business days after the employee begins work. You cannot specify which documents you will accept from an employee, such as a driver's license and Social Security card. Instead, simply show the list of acceptable documents on the back of the *I-9 Form* to your employee and allow him/her to choose which verifying documents to record. Record the information accurately and on the correct portion of the *I-9 Form*.

Section 3: You fill out Section 3 only when updating or reverifying employment eligibility. You must reverify employment eligibility of employees on or before the expiration date noted in Section 1 of the *I-9 Form*. Reverification is necessary only for expiring work authorization documents, not documents such as a driver's license.

Acceptable documentation of identity and employment eligibility is listed on the back of the *I-9 Form*. If you are shown only one document, it must be on "List A." If it is not on List A, you must instead see one document from "List B" and one document from "List C." You may choose to keep photocopies of the documents shown to you, but doing so does not eliminate the requirement of writing the information on the *I-9 Form* itself.

If an employee has the required verification of eligibility to work, it is illegal to discriminate against him/her on the basis of national origin, citizenship status, or future expiration date of verifying documents.

If employees are authorized to work, but are unable to present the required documentation at the time of hire, you still may hire them. However, within three days of being hired, employees must give you a receipt demonstrating that they have applied for the required documents. They must show you the actual documents within 90 days.

Keep completed *I–9 Forms* for all employees in a common file rather than in each employee's personnel file, for easy access during an audit by immigration or labor officials.

The United States Citizenship and Immigration Service (USCIS) makes available a *Handbook for Employers* (publication #M–274) that you can obtain by contacting your local USCIS office. Look for its listing in your local telephone directory under "Department of Homeland Security" in the U.S. Government listings. You may also download the *Handbook* on the USCIS website at ***http://uscis.gov/graphics/lawsregs/handbook/hand_emp.pdf***.

The USCIS Office of Special Counsel has established a toll–free Employer Hotline at (800) 255–8155 to provide pre–recorded information about complying with employment–related immigration laws. The hotline also has a fax–on–demand feature that allows callers to enter their fax numbers and receive government forms and other information on a variety of subjects quickly. You may also contact the department by writing to:

Office of Special Counsel for Immigration Related
Unfair Employment Practices
P.O. Box 27728
Washington, DC 20038–7728

 For more information, review the sample *I-9 Form* on the CD that comes with this product.

Workers' Compensation Documents

California Labor Code Section 3551 requires that all new employees receive a written notice informing them of their rights and obligations regarding workers' compensation. Give new employees the *Rights to Workers' Compensation Benefits and How to Obtain Them* notice at the time of hire, or by the end of the employee's first pay period. This written notice is in addition to the posting required by law. It contains generic information, so you'll need to add some information on a separate sheet regarding your own carrier, claims adjuster, etc. The notice is designed simply to inform the employee and does not need to be filled out or returned to you.

You can obtain the notice:

- As part of the California Chamber's **Required Notices Kit**. For more information, call (800) 331–8877 or visit our online store at **http://www.calchamberstore.com**;

- Individually, in packets of 25, from the California Chamber. For more information, call (800) 331–8877 or visit our online store; or

- By asking your workers' compensation carrier for its version of the written notice.

 The California Chamber's version of the notice is available in English and Spanish and has been approved by the Division of Workers' Compensation.

Predesignating a Personal Physician or Chiropractor

The written notice you use to inform employees of their rights and obligations regarding workers' compensation must contain a form for the employee to predesignate a personal physician or chiropractor, from whom they may elect to receive care if they suffer an injury covered by workers' compensation. The designated caregiver must:

- Be licensed;
- Have previously directed the employee's medical treatment;
- Possess the employee's medical records, including medical history; and
- Accept the predesignation.

If your company provides occupational medical treatment through a certified health care organization (HCO), you must furnish a personal physician designation form, such as the one on the CD that comes with this product, to every employee at the time of hire and at least annually thereafter.

Your employee must:

- Fill out the form by specifying the name, address and telephone number of the designated physician or chiropractor; and
- Secure the acceptance of the health care provider.

Once your employee completes the form, forward it to your workers' compensation insurance carrier promptly. Keep a copy of the completed form in the employee's private medical record file. If the employee subsequently wishes to designate a new personal physician:

1. Have him/her fill out a new form;
2. Forward the original form to your carrier;
3. Keep a copy in the employee's private medical record file; and
4. Clearly mark "Void" on the old form so there is no confusion about which form is current and valid.

For help with controlling workers' compensation costs, see the California Chamber's ***Managing Workers' Comp and Safety in California***.To purchase a copy of the book, call (800) 331–8877, or visit our online store at ***http:// www.calchamberstore.com***.

For more information, review the sample *Personal Physician or Personal Chiropractor Predesignation Form* on the CD that comes with this product.

Disability Insurance Documents

California's Employment Development Department (EDD) mandates that employers inform employees of their rights regarding State Disability Insurance (SDI) by distributing the *State Disability Insurance Provisions (Form DE 2515)* pamphlet. The pamphlet explains the benefits for which employees are eligible if they are unable to work because they are ill, injured, or hospitalized due to non-work related causes, or are disabled due to pregnancy, childbirth, or related medical conditions.

The pamphlet must be given to all new employees within five days of the date they are hired. You are also required to provide the same pamphlet to current employees who are become unable to work because they are ill, injured, or hospitalized due to non-work related causes, or are disabled due to pregnancy, childbirth, or related medical conditions. The pamphlet is designed simply to inform employees and does not need to be filled out or returned to you.

You may obtain the pamphlet from the California Chamber by calling (800) 331–8877, or visiting our online store at ***http://www.calchamberstore.com***. You may also request it directly from your local EDD office by submitting a completed Requisition for EDD Publications, or visiting EDD's website at ***http://www.edd.ca.gov/ formpub.htm***. For more information, contact your local EDD office, listed in the State Government section of your local telephone directory.

Health Insurance and Other Employee Benefits

There currently is no law requiring employers to provide health insurance coverage for their employees. Federal laws, such as COBRA, ERISA and HIPAA, as well as California's Cal–COBRA law, affect the way in which employers that choose to offer health insurance plans and other employee benefits must administer those plans. Laws passed in 2004 may require you to provide health insurance in the future. The California Chamber's ***2004 California Labor Law Digest*** provides a general explanation of the effect of these laws on California employers.

Unlike most of the forms in this book, forms for your health insurance plan and other employee benefits are unique to your company. Therefore, there are no corresponding forms accompanying this information. Contact your health insurance carrier or other benefit plan administrator to determine the information that new employees should receive.

COBRA Documents (Employers of 20 or More)

Employers subject to the Consolidated Omnibus Budget Reconciliation Act (COBRA) of 1985, are required to provide employees with a notice about their rights to an extension of health insurance coverage upon the occurrence of certain qualifying events. COBRA applies to all employers with 20 or more employees, including part-time and full-time employees, regardless of whether all employees participate in the group health insurance plan. You are considered as having normally employed fewer than 20 employees during a calendar year if you had fewer than 20 employees on at least 50% of the working days that year. If you are part of a multi-employer plan, check with your insurance agent to determine COBRA applicability.

You may use two different forms, depending on the location of your employees, because California law extends the continuation period to 36 months for all California employees and their dependents who experience a qualifying event. Give the appropriate *Initial Notice of COBRA Rights* form, on the CD that comes with this product, to employees at the time of hire, or when they become covered by a plan subject to COBRA:

- Use the *Initial Notice of COBRA Rights (California)* for employees residing in California

- Use the *Initial Notice of COBRA Rights (Outside California)* for employees residing outside California

Send a separate copy of the appropriate notice to the spouse of a married employee, preferably by registered mail.

If a covered employee gets married, the new spouse should receive an initial COBRA notice (preferably by mail) when he/she becomes covered. In an Advisory Opinion, the U.S. Department of Labor (DOL) has indicated that an *Initial Notice of COBRA Rights,* mailed via first-class mail and addressed to both the employee and spouse, is adequate if you understand that they reside in the same household. If not, then provide separate notices. You must furnish all employees and spouses covered by a plan subject to COBRA with a notice of their rights under COBRA.

COBRA notices must comply with the federal Health Insurance Portability and Accountability Act (HIPAA). For more information about HIPAA, see the chapter on COBRA, HIPAA and the Employee Retirement Income Security Act (ERISA) in the California Chamber's **2004 California Labor Law Digest**.

The initial COBRA information also must be included in the group health plan's summary plan description (SPD). If the employee is married, provide a separate copy of the initial notice to the covered spouse. It is recommended that the spouse's notice be sent directly to the spouse. The employee keeps the initial COBRA notice.

COBRA is a complex area of the law and legislation adopted in California in 2002, made significant changes in COBRA and Cal–COBRA benefits. The California Chamber's **2004 California Labor Law Digest** has a full chapter detailing COBRA requirements and coverage. To purchase a copy of the book, call (800) 331–8877, or visit our online store at ***http://www.calchamberstore.com***.

The IRS has COBRA and HIPAA resources available for employers or plan administrators responsible for plan activities at (202) 622–6080. You may also obtain more information by writing or calling the:

Pension and Welfare Benefits Administration
Room N5625
U.S. Department of Labor
200 Constitution Avenue NW
Washington, DC 20210
(202) 219–8776

For more information, review the sample *Initial Notice of COBRA Rights (California)* and sample *Initial Notice of COBRA Rights (Outside California)* on the CD that comes with this product.

Cal–COBRA (Employers of 2–20)

Under a California law effective in 1998, group health and disability carriers must provide COBRA–like insurance continuation benefits for employers of two to 19 employees who offer health/disability insurance. These employers must comply with the California Continuation Benefits Replacement Act (Cal–COBRA). Cal–COBRA places health insurance continuation requirements on small employers similar to what is required under the federal COBRA laws discussed previously. It also requires insurance carriers to provide continuation of benefits if the employee or a qualified beneficiary loses coverage as a result of a qualifying event. Qualifying events that entitle employees/beneficiaries to coverage are:

- The death of the covered employee or subscriber;

- The termination or reduction of hours of the covered employee's or subscriber's employment;

- Divorce or legal separation of the covered employee's spouse;

- Loss of dependent status by a dependent enrolled in the group benefit plan; or

- With respect to a dependent only, the covered employee's or subscriber's eligibility for coverage under Medicare.

Termination for gross misconduct does not constitute a qualifying event.

Employees with health/disability insurance through their employer (of two to 19 employees) must be notified of their rights under Cal–COBRA. Church plans that are not subject to COBRA became subject to state continuation coverage requirements in 2000. Consequently, churches with group health plans must follow state–mandated continuation coverage requirements, as well as California's pre–existing condition coverage provisions, which are more generous than HIPAA.

The initial Cal–COBRA notice must be provided by the health/disability insurer. Additionally, the notice must be included in plan disclosures and plan evidence of coverage. This aspect of Cal–COBRA differs from the federal COBRA requirements, which places the notification burden on you. However, it is important for employers covered by Cal–COBRA to contact their insurers to verify that all employees and qualified beneficiaries are notified of their rights to elect continuation coverage under this new state law. No sample notification is included in this book as there is no legal requirement for you to provide the notification to the employee.

You are responsible for certain notification requirements when one of the qualifying events listed previously occurs and when a group plan terminates. These requirements and their accompanying forms are discussed in "Notice of COBRA Rights" in Chapter 8, page 176. Because the burden of Cal–COBRA falls mainly on your insurer, it is wise to contact your insurer with any questions you may have about this law.

Health Benefits Documents

Only use the *HIPAA Questionnaire*— whose official IRS title is *Questionnaire for Crediting Certain Categories of Prior Plan Benefits* — on the CD that comes with this product, if you receive a *Certificate of Group Health Plan Coverage* from a new group health plan participant and he/she wishes to ask the prior plan that issued the certificate for additional information about the prior benefits. The questionnaire can be used by you or your plan administrator. HIPAA limits the extent to which group health plans may subject new employees to pre–existing condition limitations.

The following steps will help you complete the health benefit documents discussed in this section:

1. Upon receipt of a *Certificate of Group Health Plan Coverage*, you or the plan administrator fill out the *HIPAA Questionnaire* as completely as possible. Leave question six for the prior employer or plan administrator to complete.

2. You or your plan administrator send(s) the *HIPAA Questionnaire* to the former employer or plan administrator to request information about the employee's prior coverage.

3. Place a copy of the *HIPAA Questionnaire* in the employee's personnel file.

For more information about this complex new federal law, see the California Chamber's ***2004 California Labor Law Digest***.

Reporting New Employees to State

Federal law requires all employers to report information on newly hired and rehired employees a designated state agency with 20 days of hire. State agencies use the reported information to:

- Locate parents, in conjunction with child support records;

- Establish new or enforce existing child support orders; and

- Detect and prevent erroneous workers' compensation and unemployment payments.

The federal law is enforced through the department in each state responsible for employment issues. In California, employers use the *Report of New Employee(s) (Form DE 34)* to submit the required information to the EDD's New Employee Registry.

You must report all employees, regardless of age or projected wages, including those who work less than a full day, are part-time employees, are seasonal employees, or discontinue their employment before the 20th day of employment. Individuals are considered new hires on the first day they perform services for wages (i.e., first day of work). A rehire occurs when the employment relationship ended and the returning individual is required to submit a new *W-4 Form - Employee's Withholding Allowance Certificate* to you. You may report all employees who were hired within the same 20-day period on a single form.

You must report the following employee information to EDD:

- First name, middle initial and last name;

- Social Security number (SSN);

- Home address; and

- Start-of-work date.

You must also include the following employer information with your report to EDD:

- Business name and address;

- California Employer Account number;

- Federal Employer Identification number (FEIN); and

- Contact person's name and telephone number.

You may choose to report information to EDD using any of the following forms:

- *Report of New Employee(s) (Form DE 34)*, on the CD that comes with this product;

- Copy of the employee's *W–4 Form* (see "Tax Documents" on page 113);

- Alternate equivalent form; or

- Electronic or magnetic media. For more information about reporting by these means, contact EDD's Magnetic Media Unit at (916) 651-6945.

For more information about reporting new or rehired employees, contact EDD's New Employee Registry Hotline at (916) 657–0529, or contact your local EDD Employment Tax Customer Service office.

You may obtain a copy of the *Report of New Employee(s) (Form DE 34)* on EDD's website at ***http://www.edd.ca.gov***, or request the form by contacting EDD at:

Employment Development Department
P.O. Box 997016, MIC 23
West Sacramento, CA 95799–7016
(916) 657–0529
Fax: (916) 255–0951

Multi–state Employers

If you are a multi–state employer, you may elect to report, via electronic or magnetic media, all newly hired employees to one of the states in which you have employees. Employers who choose to report via electronic or magnetic media must submit two monthly transmissions that are not less than 12 or more than 16 days apart.

 For more information, review the sample *Report of New Employee(s) (Form DE 34)* on the CD that comes with this product.

Independent Contractors

The New Employee Registry program has been expanded to include independent contractors. Anyone doing business in the state (called a "service-recipient") is required to file a report with EDD when he/she hires an independent contractor (called a "service-provider") who is paid more than $600 in any year.

You are required to make your report on EDD's *Report of Independent Contractor(s) (Form DE 542) and* include the following information:

- The full name and SSN of the service-provider;

- The service-recipient's name, business name, address and telephone number;

- The service-recipient's FEIN, California Employer Account number, SSN, or other identifying number as required by the EDD in consultation with the Franchise Tax Board;

- The date the contract is executed, or if no contract, the date payments in the aggregate first equal or exceed $600;

- The total dollar amount of the contract, if any; and

- The contract expiration date.

The report is available on EDD's website at **http://www.edd.ca.gov/de542.pdf**. Mail or fax the completed report to:

Employment Development Department
P.O. Box 997350, MIC 99
Sacramento, CA 95899-7350
Fax: (916) 255-3211

When hiring a large number of independent contractors, you may send the information via magnetic media. For more information, contact EDD's Magnetic Media Unit at (916) 651-6945.

 For more information, review the sample *Report of Independent Contractor(s) (Form DE 542)* on the CD that comes with this product.

Sexual Harassment Information Sheet

Sexual harassment training must be part of your new employee orientation and training program. In addition to employees, California's FEHA also protects independent contractors from workplace harassment. Although California law does not specifically require that independent contractors receive sexual harassment information sheets, it's prudent to provide them to independent contractors. This practice ensures that independent contractors are aware of your anti–harassment and reporting policies, including their obligation not to engage in harassing conduct.

Every California employee must receive a sexual harassment information sheet at the time of hire. For current employees who have not received the information sheet, consider placing one in the employee's paycheck envelope to ensure that the employee has received a copy. The employee keeps the information sheet.

You may design a sexual harassment information sheet that complies with the law, or use the California Chamber's sexual harassment information sheet, *Sexual Harassment Hurts Everyone*. This information sheet:

- Complies with the letter and spirit of the law;
- Emphasizes internal resolution of discrimination and harassment;
- Minimizes references to litigation;
- Is available in English and Spanish; and
- Is approved by the DFEH.

You may order the information sheet from the California Chamber in packets of 25 by calling (800) 331–8877, or visiting our online store at ***http:// www.calchamberstore.com***. Each packet comes with information on how to fully comply with the law, as well as a sample complaint procedure and harassment policy.

You are required to prepare a description of your company's process for handling sexual harassment complaints, to be included on the information sheet. To assist you with sexual harassment prevention or training for employees and managers, the California Chamber publishes ***Managing to Avoid Sexual Harassment Liability***, which contains:

- A step–by–step guide to establishing a sexual harassment prevention policy;
- Information regarding training for your staff; and
- A complete investigation procedure.

This product's emphasis is on defusing explosive situations, documenting and settling complaints within the company and preventing lawsuits.

Also available is a four–part video, ***Sexual Harassment: Serious Business***, targeting your entire staff in a series of real–life job situations in which:

- Employees learn how to prevent harassment from occurring and to report it to management if it does;
- Management learns to:

– Recognize sexual harassment;

– React quickly to claims;

– Understand the personal and company liability involved; and

– Conduct a thorough and effective investigation.

To order these products, call the California Chamber at (800) 331–8877, or visit our online store at ***http://www.calchamberstore.com***.

Emergency Contact Information

Although not required by law, it is a good practice to keep emergency contact information available in case your employee is injured and unable to give important medical information or tell you who to call.

Have each employee complete an *Emergency Information* form at the time of hire. Keep the information current by requiring that employees update their information once a year. Keep emergency information in a readily accessible location, such as in a binder near your personnel files. Although keeping emergency information in personnel files is acceptable, storing it in a separate binder allows for quick access and convenience when updating information.

 For more information, review the sample *Emergency Information* form on the CD that comes with this product.

Receipt of Handbook and At–Will Statement

Although not required by law, have every employee who receives a copy of your employee handbook read and sign a receipt. Use the sample *Confirmation of Receipt Including At-will Language Policy* on the CD that comes with this product to prevent future problems when enforcing your employment policies and procedures. Documenting your employees' receipt of your at-will employment statement can be part of an effective defense if you face litigation in the future.

Employees sign and date the form after receiving an employee handbook and, preferably, after reviewing the policies with their supervisors. After they have reviewed your employee handbook at the time of hire, have employees sign the receipt. Have current employees sign the receipt any time you make a revision to the handbook. Keep each employee's receipt in his/her personnel file.

Why You Need an Employee Handbook

The benefits of developing and maintaining an employee handbook include:

- Establishing valuable legal protections;
- Providing a useful resource for new employee orientation;
- Serving to educate supervisors and managers; and
- Promoting open communication and eliminating confusion and ambiguity.

The California Supreme Court has made it clear that California employers have the right to unilaterally terminate or change policies contained in their employee handbooks without having to be concerned about violating an implied contract of employment.

The California Chamber has designed a simple and inexpensive method to help you create your own employee handbook. The information and sample policies in ***Employee Handbook: How to Write One for Your Company***, allow you to choose those policies that best fit your company's needs. The handbook is available in software or hard copy. You can order it by calling (800) 331–8877, or visiting the California Chamber store at ***http://www.calchamberstore.com***.

 For more information, review the sample *Confirmation of Receipt Including At-will Language Policy* on the CD that comes with this product.

Property Return Agreement

There is no legal requirement that you have a property return agreement. However, if you issue uniforms, tools, or other equipment to employees and want those items returned, have employees sign the form. Although you may have to resort to small claims court to have your property returned, at least you have a written acknowledgment that the employee received your property and agreed to return it.

 Uniforms required by an employer, as well as tools necessary to perform a job, must be provided and maintained by the employer. However, an employee earning at least twice the minimum wage may be required to provide and maintain hand tools and equipment customarily required by the trade or craft, except for any protective equipment and safety devices on tools or equipment regulated by Cal/OSHA.

Have your employee sign the agreement at the time you issue company property to him/her. Update the agreement every time new property is issued, including replacement property. Keep the original agreement in the employee's personnel file.

For more information, review the sample *Property Return Agreement* on the CD that comes with this product.

Wage Deductions for Unreturned Property

The California courts have ruled that no deductions may be made from employees' final wages even though they have not returned your business property. Employers are subject to fines for such deductions. However, employees are more likely to return your property if, at the time of termination, they are reminded of the written agreement they signed agreeing to return the property. It is possible to deduct from wages the value of some property entrusted to employees through a somewhat cumbersome bonding process contained in California Labor Code Sections 400–410. For more information, contact the local office of the Division of Labor Standards Enforcement (DLSE), listed in your local telephone directory under "Department of Industrial Relations" in the State Government section.

Confidentiality Agreement

You are not legally required to ask employees to sign a confidentiality agreement. However, you often must give certain employees access to confidential information in order that they may do their jobs. Concern naturally arises as to what the employee may do with the confidential information, particularly after the termination of employment. Without an agreement, former employees could use your confidential client lists, trade secrets, formulas, or techniques to compete against you, their former employer, making them formidable business competitors.

It is important to understand the limited protection afforded by an agreement with employees not to compete with their employers after termination of the employment relationship. California Business and Professional Code Section 16600 invalidates provisions in employment contracts or covenants not to compete that prohibit employees from working for a competitor after completion of their employment or impose a penalty for doing so, unless the provisions are necessary to protect the your trade secrets.

 A trade secret is information, including a formula, pattern, program, customer list, device, technique, or process that:

- Derives independent economic value from not being generally known to the public or others who could obtain economic value from it; and

- Is the subject of reasonable efforts under the circumstances to maintain its secrecy.

In other words, other businesses must be unaware of the information and be able to put that information, if it were known to them, to beneficial use.

Prepare your confidentiality agreement based on the type of confidential information to which an employee might have access. The sample *Confidentiality Agreement* on the CD that comes with this product is a standard agreement that applies to most businesses. However, it is strongly advised that you have the agreement reviewed by legal counsel to ensure that it protects the information within your company that you need to protect.

At the start of employment, have your employee read the agreement carefully and sign it. It is a good idea to encourage and answer questions from the employee as to what the agreement might cover, to ensure that he/she fully understands the types of information involved. Keep the original agreement in the employee's personnel file and give a copy to the employee, if requested.

 For more information, review the sample *Confidentiality Agreement* on the CD that comes with this product.

Arbitration Agreements

For the purpose of avoiding protracted and costly court litigation, some employers request or require applicants to sign agreements to arbitrate disputes that arise out of the employment relationship or its termination. There has been considerable federal and state court litigation, however, over the effort to require acceptance of such agreements by applicants and employees, as well as their enforcement.

 Because of the complexities that have arisen, seek legal counsel before using arbitration agreements with applicants or employees. Keep the completion of arbitration agreements separate from any other task in the hiring process.

 The sample *Employment Application - Long Form* and sample *Employment Application - Short Form* on the CD that comes with this product do not contain arbitration agreement clauses.

The Law Explained

The courts have taken important steps forward in the development of arbitration as an enforceable element of human resource policy. In a landmark decision under the Federal Arbitration Act (FAA), *Circuit City Stores v. Adams,* the United States Supreme Court held that an employer can enforce arbitration agreements that require the employee to take all employment–related disputes to arbitration rather than to court.[1]

After deciding *Circuit City,* the Supreme Court took up the thornier question of whether arbitration agreements limit rights under antidiscrimination and other federal laws that protect employees. In *Equal Opportunity Commission v. Waffle House, Inc.,* the Court held that an arbitration agreement between an employer and employee for employment–related disputes does not preclude the EEOC from seeking judicial relief on the employee's behalf.[2]

In its decision in *Armendariz v. Foundation Health Psychcare Services,* the California Supreme Court provided important guidance for employers on the underlying question of exactly what terms must be included in an arbitration agreement for it to be enforceable.[3] The Court held that mandatory arbitration of employment disputes may be a lawful condition of employment if:

- The arbitrator is neutral and provides a written arbitration decision;

- Adequate discovery is allowed, including a fair and simple method for the employee to get information necessary for his/her claim;

- The arbitration agreement does not limit the employee's potential damages to less than what could be awarded in court, including punitive damages and attorney's fees;

- The arbitration agreement does not require the employee to pay any expense the employee would not be required to pay if he/she were free to bring the action in court. For example, an employer may not require employees to share in the cost of the arbitrator, because no such fee sharing is required in a court of law; and

- The arbitration agreement is not overly harsh or one–sided. An agreement generally would not be enforceable if it requires employees to arbitrate all claims, but leaves the employer free to pursue claims, such as trade secret injunctions, against the employee in court. In practical terms, this requirement imposes an important limitation on the employer's freedom of decision in that both parties must submit disputes to arbitration.

---

1. *Circuit City Stores v. Adams,* 532 U.S. 105, 121 S.Ct. 1302 (2001)

2. *Equal Opportunity Commission v. Waffle House, Inc.,* 534 U.S. 279 (2002)

3. *Armendariz v. Foundation Health Psychcare Services,* 24 Cal. 4th 83 (2000)

In 2002, the 9th Circuit Court of Appeals issued a decision that affirmed its willingness to enforce arbitration agreements that meet the standards established by the California Supreme Court in the Armendariz case.[4] In one case, the court enforced a mandatory arbitration policy where the employee acknowledged receipt of the policy, but did not exercise the chance to opt-out. The court rejected the argument that the employee should not be bound because he did not expressly agree to do so.[5]

New for 2004 Finally, the 9th Circuit agreed with the California Supreme Court in that requiring employees to sign agreements to arbitrate Title VII discrimination claims as a condition of employment does not itself constitute unlawful discrimination.[6] Although the court ruled out discrimination, it left open the related question of unlawful retaliation by employers. What remains an important issue for employers is whether termination of an employee or rejection of an applicant for refusing to sign such an agreement constitutes unlawful retaliation prohibited by Title VII. Although the 9th Circuit noted that, if employers may rightfully require employees to arbitrate all employment claims, it makes no sense to treat enforcing that right as retaliation. The Court permitted the EEOC to present its position on the retaliation question to the lower court, so that issue is currently awaiting decision. [7]

What You Should Do

The net result of these decisions is that arbitration agreements, if carefully drafted, are likely to be considered enforceable by the courts. However, their effectiveness is limited because some rights remain enforceable in administrative proceedings or in court enforcement actions brought by regulatory agencies, such as the EEOC, on behalf of the employee. Also, the possible liability for refusing to hire a candidate or terminating an employee who reject mandatory arbitration of Title VII cases continues until the issue is ruled upon.

Orientation and Training

The introductory period for any new employee is typically a challenging time for both the employee and his/her supervisor. Often the attention given to the task of training at this time sets the employee on the road to success, or allows the supervisor to identify and deal with a poor hiring decision. The following suggestions can help you manage employee performance effectively and provide you with documentation tools.

---

4. *Circuit City v. Ahmed*, 383 F.3d 1198 (9th Cir., 2002)

5. *Circuit City v. Njad*, 294 F.3d 1104 (9th Cir., 2002)

6. *EEOC v. Luce, Forward, Hamilton and Scripps*, 303 F.3d 994 (9th Cir., 2002)

7. *EEOC v. Luce, Forward, Hamilton & Scripps*, (9th Cir., Sept. 30, 2003) No. 00–57222

The Law Explained

Every California workplace is required to establish, implement and maintain an effective Injury and Illness Prevention Program (IIPP), which must include mandatory initial training on general safe and healthy work practices and, if not already trained for the position, on hazards that are specific to their jobs. Although the Cal/OSHA standard is silent on exactly when the training should occur, if a new employee who has not been trained is injured, Cal/OSHA may regard this as a failure to provide required training prior to allowing him/her to begin work. For more information on IIPPs, see the California Chamber's ***Managing Workers' Comp and Safety in California***. You can order it by calling (800) 331–8877, or visiting the California Chamber store at ***http://www.calchamberstore.com***.

Any employer who exposes, or may expose, an employee to any amount of hazardous substances must train the employee concerning this exposure in order to comply with the requirements of the hazard communication standard.

Almost all California employers must maintain a system to document that the required training was provided, both for the IIPP and the emergency action and fire prevention plans. The training documentation should be easily accessible if Cal/OSHA shows up for an inspection.

Negligent Training

Liability for negligent training may be found if you fail to train or improperly train an employee. Examples of negligent training include an employer failing to provide employees with:

- Proper training and/or education to perform the job safely and effectively; or

- Necessary knowledge and/or training to use a dangerous tool or instrument necessary for the job.

Examples of specific cases in which plaintiffs have prevailed on the theory of negligent training include situations where:

- A woman was assaulted and raped in a parking garage. The testimony showed that the assault could have been prevented if security agents hired to provide security for the parking garage had been properly trained;[8]

- A 16–year old employee of a rental car agency, while driving a rental car without authorization, collided with another automobile, killing two of its occupants and seriously injuring two others. The rental franchise was found negligent in

---

8. *Erickson v. Curtis Investment Co.*, 432 N.W.2d 199 (Minn. Ct. App. 1988), Aff'd 447 N.W.2d 165 (Minn. 1989)

hiring youngsters as employees, failing to properly train them and leaving them unsupervised and in sole control of the premises;[9] and

- Several plaintiffs were beaten and placed under arrest by police officers. The police department was found negligent because it had a policy of issuing blackjacks without adequate supervision or training in the use of such weapons.[10]

What You Should Do

You must review your emergency action and fire prevention plans with new employees at the time of hire. Give employees copies of the plans, which are specific to your workplace so samples are not provided in this book. If you need assistance creating these plans, refer to the California Chamber's *Cal/OSHA Basics: Written Plans and Programs*. Employers with 10 or fewer employees may communicate the plan orally to their employees and do not need to maintain a written emergency action or fire prevention plan.

If your workplace is inspected by the California Occupational Safety and Hazards Administration (Cal/OSHA), your employees are likely to be asked whether the company has an IIPP. Therefore, thoroughly reviewing your IIPP with a new employee at the time of hire is especially important to a successful inspection. It is in the best interest of you and your employee that the safety orientation take place as the employee is being introduced to the workplace and his/her job assignment. If safety is a high priority to you, it also becomes a priority to your employee. Employees who are new to the job have significantly more accidents than do employees who have been on the job for at least one year.

Provide training as often as it is required to maintain a safe workplace for employees. In addition to the general and job–specific safety orientation training, employees should receive training:

- Before beginning an unfamiliar assignment;

- If new equipment or hazards enter the workplace; and

- Upon discovery of any new or previously unrecognized hazard.

See the *Individual Employee Training Documentation - Initial Safety Training* form on the CD that comes with this product for a list of activities to include in a new employee's basic safety training.

---

9. *O'Boyle v. Avis Rent–a–Car, Inc.*, 435 N.Y.S.2d 296 (1981)

10. *O'Boyle v. Avis Rent–a–Car, Inc.*, 435 N.Y.S.2d 296 (1981)

Specific training requirements are outlined throughout Title 8 of the California Codes and Regulations. The California Chamber's **Managing Workers' Comp and Safety in California**, contains a summary of these requirements. You can order it by calling (800) 331–8877, or visiting the California Chamber store at ***http:// www.calchamberstore.com***. For additional Cal/OSHA information, contact your local Cal/OSHA consultation office, listed in your local telephone directory under "Department of Industrial Relations" in the State Government section.

Providing New Employee Orientation

Provide all new employees with an orientation session. Include an introduction to your employee handbook and a review of other important employee policies and behavioral expectations as part of the session. It is also a good time to emphasize the at–will nature of employment and have the employee sign the *Confirmation of Receipt Including At-will Language Policy* form on the CD that comes with this product. For more information see "Employment At–Will" in Chapter 2, page 13.

Also use the opportunity to review your company's benefit programs, even though employees may not be immediately eligible for them. Cover the eligibility requirements and what employees may need to do upon becoming eligible to enroll. Include an information sheet summarizing employee benefits and eligibility requirements.

The sample *Employee Orientation Checklist* on the CD that comes with this product can provide important documentation in a later lawsuit or investigation by showing that you took all steps necessary to comply with the law. Use the sample *Employee Orientation Checklist* on the CD that comes with this product to verify that your new employees:

- Filled out and returned the required forms;

- Participated in orientation;

- Received all training required by your company; and

- Had an opportunity to ask questions about anything they did not completely understand.

As employees go through orientation and training, have them initial each item as it is completed. When all items on the checklist have been completed and initialed, have the employee and supervisor sign the form. Keep each employee's orientation checklist/verification in his/her personnel file.

Documenting Training

Develop a training checklist for the essential functions of each job, as found in its job description and use the checklist to record the date that new employees demonstrate competence in performing each function. This practice assures that each new employee is given the training needed to be successful and that every employee receives the same attention to training.

What Forms and Checklists Do I Use to Get New Employees Started Right?

The following table describes forms and checklists associated with getting new employees started right.

 You can find these forms on the CD that comes with this product.

Table 14. Required Forms' Checklists and Pamphlets

Form/Checklist Name	What do I use it for?	When do I use it?	Who fills it out?	Where does it go?
California Employee's Withholding Allowance Certificate (Form DE 4)	All employees	Before employee's first pay date	Employee fills out form	Keep the form in the employee's personnel record. If you sent the original to payroll, keep a copy of the form.
HIPAA Questionnaire	To respond to a Certificate of Group Health Plan Coverage (a HIPAA Certificate) from a new group health plan participant	On the day the employee enrolls for the benefit	Question 6: prior employer or plan administrator. The rest of the form: current employer or plan administrator.	Send the HIPAA Questionnaire to the prior employer or plan administrator. Keep a copy of the questionnaire in your personnel records.

Table 14. Required Forms' Checklists and Pamphlets

Form/Checklist Name	What do I use it for?	When do I use it?	Who fills it out?	Where does it go?
I-9 Form	To verify the immigration status of all employees	**Section 1:** At the time of hire **Section 2:** Within three business days after the employee's first day of work **Section 3:** On or before the expiration date in Section 1	**Section 1:** Employee fills out **Section 2:** You fill out **Section 3:** You fill out if necessary for updating or re-verifying	Keep the forms for all employees in a common file rather than separate personnel records
Initial Notice of COBRA Rights (California)	All employers with 20 or more employees This notice must be included in the group health plan's *Summary Plan Description*	On the day the employee enrolls for the benefit	You do then give to employee and beneficiaries residing in California	Send a copy of the notice to the spouse of a married employee, preferably by registered mail. Keep a record of the mailing and/or distribution at hire of this notice to both employee and spouse on the Hiring Checklist.

Table 14. Required Forms' Checklists and Pamphlets

Form/Checklist Name	What do I use it for?	When do I use it?	Who fills it out?	Where does it go?
Initial Notice of COBRA Rights (Outside California)	All employers with 20 or more employees This notice must be included in the group health plan's Summary Plan Description	On the day the employee enrolls for the benefit	You do then give to employee and beneficiaries residing outside California	Send a copy of the notice to the spouse of a married employee, preferably by registered mail. Keep a record of the mailing and/or distribution at hire of this notice to both employee and spouse on the Hiring Checklist.
Personal Physician or Personal Chiropractor Predesignation Form	To notify employees of their right to elect medical treatment by their personal physician or chiropractor	Give it to the employee at the time of hire	The employee	Keep a copy in the employee's personnel file
Report of Independent Contractor(s) (Form DE 542)	All new independent contractors The District Attorney uses the information in this form to locate parents who owe child support funds	As soon as possible after signing the contract	You do	Mail or fax the form to: Employment Development Department P.O. Box 997350 MIC 99 Sacramento, CA 95899-7350 Fax: (916) 255-3211

Table 14. Required Forms' Checklists and Pamphlets

Form/Checklist Name	What do I use it for?	When do I use it?	Who fills it out?	Where does it go?
Report of New Employee(s) (Form DE 34)	All new employees 💡 The District Attorney uses the information in this form to locate parents who owe child support funds	Within 20 days of hire	You do	Mail or fax the form to: Employment Development Department P.O. Box 997016, MIC 23 West Sacramento, CA 95799-7016 Fax: (916) 255-0951
Rights to Workers' Compensation Benefits	To provide notice to employees of their right to workers' compensation benefits should they sustain an on-the-job injury	Give it to all new employees at hire and again to any employee who is injured at work	The employee fills out the Personal Physician or Personal Chiropractor form; the rest is informational	Put the predesignation form in the employee's regular personnel file. The employee keeps the rest of the brochure for reference
Sexual Harassment Hurts Everyone	This form describes the problem and the penalties of sexual harassment	Whenever you hire a new employee, or engage an independent contractor, etc.	No filling out needed	Give it to your workers and make sure they understand its contents

Table 14. Required Forms' Checklists and Pamphlets

Form/Checklist Name	What do I use it for?	When do I use it?	Who fills it out?	Where does it go?
State Disability Insurance Provisions (Form DE 2515)	To advise employee of SDI benefits	All new employees and any employee going on disability leave	NA	NA
W-4 Form - Employee's Withholding Allowance Certificate	All employees	Before employee's first pay date	Employee fills out form	Keep the form in the employee's personnel record. If you sent the original to payroll, keep a copy of the form.

Table 15. Recommended Forms and Checklists

Form/Checklist Name	What do I use it for?	When do I use it?	Who fills it out?	Where does it go?
Confidentiality Agreement	Obtaining employee acknowledge-ment that there is information necessary for his/her job that he/she may not disclose	At the time of hire or change in duties of an employee	You prepare the agreement You should have the agreement reviewed by an attorney. Employee signs the agreement.	The original agreement should go in the employee's personnel record. Provide the employee a copy.
Confirmation of Receipt Including At-will Language Policy	Use to document that the employee has received and understands your company policies	When hiring a new employee, or when you make a signifi-cant change to your handbook	The employee signs it	Keep in each employee's personnel file

Table 15. Recommended Forms and Checklists

Form/Checklist Name	What do I use it for?	When do I use it?	Who fills it out?	Where does it go?
Emergency Information	Recording important medical information and contacts in case of an emergency	At the time of hire. Keep the form updated throughout employment.	Employee fills the form out	Keep emergency information readily accessible. You may keep the forms in your personnel records, but you might want to use a separate binder for quick access.
Employee Orientation Checklist	Tracking completed orientation tasks	In the first weeks of employment	Manager	Keep in the employee's personnel file
Hiring Checklist	Tracking completion of recommended and required hiring procedures and forms	During the recruiting and hiring process	Manager or other person in charge of hiring employees	Keep in the employee's personnel file

Table 15. Recommended Forms and Checklists

Form/Checklist Name	What do I use it for?	When do I use it?	Who fills it out?	Where does it go?
Individual Employee Training Documentation - Initial Safety Training	To document the first training provided to an employee	When you hire someone, reassign someone, or identify a previously unknown hazard	You do	Keep the certificate in the employee's personnel file. Provide a copy of the certificate to the employee if requested.
Property Return Agreement	Obtaining employee acknowledge that he/she has received property of yours (tools, uniforms, etc.) and agrees to return the property	When your property is issued to the employee	Employee signs the form	Keep the original agreement in your personnel records

Chapter 6

Evaluating Employee Performance

Regular performance evaluations can improve employee performance by creating a consistent and formal setting in which you can advise employees about:

- How they are doing;

- How their performance supports the company's goals; and

- Steps they can take to advance their careers.

Performance evaluations also can lay the groundwork for subsequent disciplinary action if identified performance problems continue. Assessment of employees' performance is also used to select candidates for promotion and as a basis for compensation decisions.

Informal performance evaluations occur frequently in the work environment. Supervisors usually make both negative and positive comments to their employees on a regular basis as part of the work process. A formal performance evaluation is conducted in an interview setting and includes a review of the employee's performance during a certain period of time. Formal performance evaluations provide the:

- Supervisor with an accurate and complete picture of an employee's performance; and

- Employee with information he/she can use to:

    - Do a better job in meeting the organizations goals;

    - Develop potential to assume higher positions and responsibility;

    - Work on areas that are unsatisfactory;

    - Receive recognition for duties that are done well; and

    - Ideally, communicate concerns and problems.

A useful tool for management, information learned in performance evaluations has an effect on:

- Recruitment and hiring by revealing when the wrong people are being hired and that hiring interviews are not finding qualified employees;

- Training and development by revealing that employees are being poorly trained and are unprepared to do their jobs to the level required to meet organizational goals;

- Decisions regarding compensation, promotions, demotions and staffing; and

- The budgeting process, because the results of performance evaluations may suggest a change in allocation of money and human resources.

Finally, performance evaluations also have a huge effect on motivating employees. They ensure that employees:

- Understand the level of performance necessary to meet job requirements;

- Recognize how their performance measures up to job requirements; and

- Receive proper recognition for good outcomes.

Performance evaluations also can help employees identify performance areas needing improvement and provides them with an opportunity to communicate problems and issues of concern to the supervisor.

Employers face negative consequences for failing to periodically assess performance. Unidentified poor performers lower productivity and may be responsible for customer dissatisfaction, product defects, acts of sabotage, increased conflict and poor morale in the workplace. Without performance evaluations to document these issues, it is difficult to defend against discrimination claims and wrongful termination suits.

Conducting and Documenting Periodic Training

Conducting periodic training is a way to:

- Improve employee productivity;

- Increase morale; and

- Ensure that employees' skills are maintained.

Document the content of the training and the names of employees participating in all training and educational programs. By monitoring employees' work performance, managers and supervisors can provide regular feedback regarding their on-the-job performance. Finally, document incidents of the employee's inability to perform the job properly and effectively and take corrective action.

The Law Explained

There is no legal requirement that you perform performance evaluations, except in certain highly regulated industries, such as health care. Federal and state laws prohibiting discrimination provide a basis for challenge to performance evaluations if inconsistency can be shown in the standards being measured or the ratings being given. Therefore, it is important to have all employees performing similar functions rated with the same evaluation tool and to support ratings with objective evidence whenever possible. Where ratings are based on opinion, document the basis for that opinion in the evaluation. This practice assists the supervisor during communication with the employee and later if asked to testify about the evaluation, during investigation or litigation.

What You Should Do

Use job content in developing the basis of the performance evaluation instrument. Base appraisals on performance and behavior rather than on personality traits. Provide supervisors with specific written instructions and training on how to complete appraisals. Ensure that appraisals are reviewed with the individual employees and that the employee is given the opportunity to comment and submit written comments, if appropriate. Performance evaluations may be done annually, every six months, or even every quarter. You should settle on how often employees will be evaluated and to stick to it.

Designing Performance Evaluation Tools

In an effective performance management system, company goals are reflected in position descriptions and are then distilled into evaluation criteria. Job competencies connect company goals to employee evaluations. So, it is critical that employees are evaluated based on the competencies that are most important for performing well in their jobs and for promoting the goals of the organization. Evaluation tools must be:

- **Valid** — which means that the evaluation must measure what it is intended to measure. The responsibilities for each job must be clearly stated and reflect the duties actually performed. Job responsibilities should relate directly to the job description, assuming the job description itself is accurate;

- **Reliable** — which refers to the fact that the results of evaluation must be consistent. Levels of performance must be evaluated similarly at different periods, the same level of performance by two individuals must be recognized equally and results may not be substantially influenced because employees have been rated by different evaluators;

- **Non–discriminatory** — which means the performance evaluation must support discrimination based only on performance and not on extraneous factors;

- **Free from bias** — which means that the supervisor must be unbiased, aided by an appraisal tool that has clearly defined duties and tasks; and

- **Relevant** — which means that evaluations:

  - Must be related to the job, omitting irrelevant factors; and

  - Should rate the whole job, as reviewing only parts of the job suggests to employees that only their weak points are being addressed.

Preparing Performance Evaluations

The immediate supervisor is usually the person who conducts performance evaluations because employees find an evaluation credible only if they feel that their evaluators are familiar with the tasks being evaluated. Before the evaluation period begins, the supervisor must make sure that the employee understands what is expected of him/her. The supervisor and employee should review the performance standards together and the supervisor should indicate the relative importance of each standard.

The supervisor assumes the role of a coach to help employees in the following ways:

- Identify current or potential problems that may be affecting performance;

- Generate possible solutions and map out a plan to improve performance; and

- Build on employee strengths.

Before the performance evaluation interview, the supervisor should give the employee plenty of time to prepare. This is where self–evaluation may come in handy. Letting employees rate themselves on a duplicate performance evaluation form may help them understand how they have been rated and provides them with a chance to communicate their opinions. If, during the review period, the supervisor has let employees know, on an informal basis, how they are doing, the formal evaluation interview should produce few surprises to the employee.

When preparing to meet with employees, supervisors should consider the following:

- What results do I want?

- What contribution is my employee making?

- What contribution should my employee be making?

- Is my employee working near his/her potential?

- Does my employee know clearly what is expected?

- What training, if any, does he/she need?

- What are my employee's strengths?

- How has my performance helped or hindered him/her?

Other tasks that supervisors should complete before conducting a performance evaluation review include:

- Reviewing the job factors and rating them according to their degree of importance to the job;

- Comparing employee behavior to established performance standards;

- Documenting specific behaviors that meets or exceeds the standards;

- Identifying specific areas in need of improvement;

- Determining goals and objectives for the coming review period; and

- Summarizing overall performance and developmental needs.

Conducting the Review

At the beginning of the review, the supervisor should put the employee at ease and make sure the employee understands the purpose of the review. The supervisor should then:

- Explain what information he/she used to determine performance;

- Present his/her assessment and provide positive and corrective feedback;

- Identify specific areas for improvement;

- Discuss observed behavior and get commitment to goals and objectives for the next review period;

- Be candid;

- Set specific goals; and

- Build on the employee's strengths.

Throughout the review, the supervisor should ask for the employee's opinion and try to reach a consensus about each performance rating. Give specific examples when criticizing and complementing the employee. Encourage the employee to speak and make comments on the ratings. Towards the end of the review, the supervisor should ask the employee if all concerns have been addressed and make sure he/she understands what performance areas need improving and where he/she stand in the organization's structure. Recognize that the employee may want to respond to particular points so allow sufficient time to listen to his/her concerns. Give the employee a day or more to respond to and sign the evaluation. If the employee is reluctant to sign the appraisal, explain that his/her signature reflects receipt of the form and does not necessarily indicate agreement with the contents.

Once the evaluation is completed and signed by both the evaluator and the employee, make a copy for the employee and keep the original in his/her personnel file.

Relating Performance to Compensation

Although the outcome of a performance evaluation may have an impact on an employee's future compensation, it is important to separate the performance discussion from talk of compensation changes. When the two issues are combined, the impact of the performance evaluation is often submerged in the conversation about pay. Unless you have a policy or labor contract directly linking the two, it's a good idea to make it clear to employees that performance evaluations and wage increases do not necessarily go hand in hand. Whatever your policy, include the information in your employee handbook, as well as on the performance evaluation form.

 For more information, review the sample *Performance Evaluation* on the CD that comes with this product.

What Forms and Checklists Do I Use to Evaluate Employee Performance?

The following table describes forms and checklists associated with evaluating employee performance.

 You can find these forms on the CD that comes with this product.

Table 16. Recommended Forms and Checklists

Form/ Checklist Name	What do I use it for?	When do I use it?	Who fills it out?	Where does it go?
Performance Evaluation	To document and provide feedback to employees about performance issues	At end of introductory period and periodically per policy (usually annually) thereafter	Supervisor	Keep in the employee's personnel file

Chapter 7

Conducting Reorganizations and Workforce Reductions

There comes a time in the history of almost every business that layoffs are necessary because of business conditions, reorganizations, merger or sale of the company or outright shutdown. Although at–will employment gives you the right to employ layoffs, there are legal ramifications. This chapter explores the notice obligations of businesses terminating substantial numbers of employees. It also suggests ways to reduce liability when making layoff decisions.

Mass Layoffs and Terminations

If you are contemplating the need to significantly change the number of individuals employed in a department, plant or your company as a whole, you must anticipate that need early enough to allow time to comply with both the federal Worker Adjustment and Retraining Notification (WARN) Act and its California equivalent: the Cal–WARN Act. In most cases, this means knowing, more than 60 days in advance:

- What you need to do;

- How you need to do it; and

- What employees and unions are impacted by these decisions.

The Law Explained

The federal WARN Act requires covered employers to provide employees, their representatives and specified government officials and agencies, with 60 days written notice prior to any mass layoffs or plant closings. Penalties, including up to 60 days back pay per employee, could be assessed for failure to provide required notice.

California's version of the WARN Act is broader in scope than the federal act is and affects more employers. California businesses have to comply with the requirements of both laws.

In many ways, the Cal–WARN Act parallels the requirements of the WARN Act, but it also imposes significantly different rules and requirements. Most importantly, the state law covers smaller employers. Also, the events that trigger obligations under the state law are somewhat different from those that trigger obligations under the federal law. Like the federal law, however, failure to give timely and proper notice can result in significant financial obligations to the affected employees, as well as fines and litigation expenses.

To quickly understand the similarities and differences between the federal and state laws and the basic requirements of each, see the chart, *Major Features of Mass Layoff and Plant Closing Laws* on the CD that comes with this product.

As the chart indicates, the two laws define different events that trigger notice obligations and differ slightly as to the parties to whom notices must be given. California employers covered by both laws must ensure compliance with the requirements of both laws. The following events trigger the notice requirement. If you are contemplating reduced activity, carefully measure your proposed action against these definitions:

- **Plant Closing** — A temporary or permanent plant closing under the federal law is a shutdown of a "single site of employment," or one or more facilities or operating units within a single site of employment, during any 30–day period at the single site of employment for 50 or more employees, excluding any part–time employees, if the shutdown results in:

  - An employment termination, other than a discharge for cause, voluntary departure, or retirement;

  - A layoff exceeding six months; or

  - A reduction in an employee's hours of work of more than 50% in each month of any six–month period.

An employment action that results in the effective cessation of production or the work performed by a unit, even if a few employees remain, is a shutdown.

Mass Layoff is defined differently under federal and state law. Compare the two definitions using the following table.

Table 17. Mass Layoff

A mass layoff under federal law is:	A mass layoff under state law is:
For a period of 30 days	For a period of 30 days
Consists of 50 or more full–time employees (provided it affects at least 33% of the work force). If 500 or more employees (excluding part–time employees) are affected, the 33% requirement does not apply.	Consists of 50 or more full– or part–time employees who have been employed by an employer for at least six months of the 12 months preceding the date on which notice is required for lack of funds or lack of work.

- **Termination** — A termination under state law is "the cessation or substantial cessation of industrial or commercial operations." The Cal–WARN Act does not give any indication as to what qualifies as a "substantial cessation" of operations. The courts will have to decide what constitutes a "substantial cessation" unless it is clarified by subsequent regulations.

- **Relocation** — A relocation under *state* law is the removal of all or substantially all industrial or commercial operations over 100 miles away. In California, you are required to give notice.

  Under the *federal* law, you don't have to give notice of a relocation if you offer to:

  – Transfer employees to a new work site within a "reasonable commuting distance," and there is less than a six month break in employment; or

  – Transfer employees to a new work site located anywhere else you conduct business and they accept that offer.

Each law contains certain limited exceptions to the 60 day notice requirement related to unforeseen circumstances, uncertain business conditions and good faith efforts to keep the business alive.

What You Should Do

Become sufficiently familiar with the federal and state laws so you'll know how far in advance you'll need to consult with legal counsel as to compliance. For more information on the content of and procedure for giving notice, see the California Chamber's *2004 California Labor Law Digest*.

Making and Documenting Layoff Decisions

With the exception of a California law restricting layoff of certain janitorial and building service personnel,[1] no law dictates how or when you decide to layoff workers. However, the process you use to select who will be laid off is subject to review as a result of federal and state laws protecting employees from unlawful discrimination and retaliation. An employee who believes he or she was selected for layoff because of membership in a protected class or participation in some protected activity may seek redress under one of those laws.

The Law Explained

Unless your layoff affects an entire unit or classification of employees, such that there is no need to differentiate and select specific individuals, you must be prepared to justify the process you used to select employees for layoff and prove that it was carried out in an objective manner.

> **Example:** If your company needs to reduce its staff of warehouse workers and the layoff disproportionately affects men over the age of 55, women, or Asians, the burden shifts to the company to prove that the selection process was neutral for those groups.

Even a single individual can allege that he or she was selected for a discriminatory reason, or in retaliation for some protected activity, such as:

- Union advocacy;

- Making safety complaints;

- Whistleblowing to a government agency;

- Protesting unlawful discrimination;

- Having a workers' compensation claim; or

- Testifying in a sexual harassment investigation.

What You Should Do

Rather than assuming that a layoff is necessary, first consider alternatives, such as reduced hours, job sharing, improving internal processes or salary and benefits cost reductions. Creative approaches such as these can save a lot of expense by:

---

1. Labor Code Sections 1060–1065

- Retaining a productive workforce;

- Avoiding recruiting costs when business picks up;

- Showing concern for staff members;

- Allowing employees to participate in matters that affect their lives; and

- Reducing unemployment insurance costs.

EDD has created a special Work Sharing Program to help you avoid mass layoffs by sharing the available work among employees. This program offers you three basic advantages by allowing you to:

- Continue providing some work to all employees, rather than laying off significant groups;

- Maintain a relationship with a trained work force against the time business returns to normal; and

- Reduce overall cost because the employees involved in the work sharing plan are receiving lower amounts in benefits–although your costs are the same as any employer with a similar unemployment tax rating.

For more information about the Work Sharing Program, contact:

Special Claims Office
P.O. Box 269058
Sacramento, CA 95826–9058
(916) 464–3300
Fax: (916) 464–3342

Preparing for a Reduction in Force

Take the following steps when preparing for a reduction in force:

1. Use the tools you have created by following the advice contained in this book.

Example: You can use the performance evaluation and employee discipline documentation tools discussed previously to assist you in making legally supportable decisions when selecting employees for layoff. Using these tools you can develop a set of objective criteria for selecting those employees to be laid off. Be sure you can clearly articulate the criteria you have selected, the reasons you selected them and show that they contain some objective content.

2. Evaluate the probable outcome for disparate impact.

Disparate impact means that, although each employee layoff selection may be based on legitimate business–related criteria, the impact on a particular protected class may provide the basis for discrimination claims.

3. If employees are represented by a union, give the union sufficient notice and a chance to bargain. Although there is normally no obligation to bargain over the decision to layoff employees (unless it is motivated solely by labor costs), there is a duty to give unions notice of the layoffs and an opportunity to bargain over the effects of the decision. For more information, see the sample *WARN Notice - Union Representatives* on the CD that comes with this product.

4. Determine whether you are subject to state and/or federal notice requirements describes in "Mass Layoffs and Terminations" on page 149. Your failure to comply with advance notice requirements can be costly. For more information, see the sample *WARN Notice - State/Local Officials* on the CD that comes with this product.

5. Make sure your managers are knowledgeable about the layoff plans, including the underlying reasons for the layoffs and what you want them to do and say.

6. Communicating with employees is an essential ingredient of sound management practice. Let employees know shortly before the layoffs that there will be some downsizing. Explain the reasons why it is necessary. Reassure the remaining employees that they are valued. For more information, see the sample *WARN Notice - Employees* on the CD that comes with this product.

7. Have final paychecks, employee notices and documentation prepared in advance. If you are offering severance packages, have the separation agreements and releases prepared by legal counsel. For more information, see "Obligations upon Termination" in Chapter 8, page 170.

What Forms and Checklists Do I Use to Conduct Reorganizations and Workforce Reductions?

The following table describes forms and checklists associated with conducting reorganizations and workforce reductions.

You can find these forms on the CD that comes with this product.

Table 18. Recommended Forms and Checklists

Form/Checklist Name	What do I use it for?	When do I use it?	Who fills it out?	Where does it go?
Major Features of Mass Layoff and Plant Closing Laws	To compare features of federal and state laws	When considering a plant closing or layoff	NA	NA
WARN Notice - Employees	To advise affected parties of impending plant closing or mass layoff	At least 60 days before a plant closing or mass layoff	You do	Keep in employee's personnel file
WARN Notice - State/Local Officials	To advise affected parties of impending plant closing or mass layoff	At least 60 days before a plant closing or mass layoff	You do	Correspondence file
WARN Notice - Union Representatives	To advise affected parties of impending plant closing or mass layoff	At least 60 days before a plant closing or mass layoff	You do	Correspondence file

Chapter 8

Disciplining and Terminating Employees

By following the recommendations outlined in this book, you will likely hire a workforce composed of capable and motivated employees. However, there are no guarantees and one of the greatest challenges for managers is making and implementing a decision to discipline or terminate an employee. This chapter assists you in making sound decisions about employee performance and behavior and helps you avoid legal pitfalls when it becomes necessary to discipline or terminate an employee.

Wrongful Termination: Limitations on At–Will Employment

As discussed in Chapter 2, the relationship of employer and employee is generally "at–will," unless you have done or agreed to something that provides greater job security. First, we'll discuss the exceptions to at–will employment created either by statute or as a result of court decisions.

Avoiding a wrongful termination lawsuit begins long before the time you decide an employee must be terminated. Each step in the employment process affects the probability that you will face a wrongful termination lawsuit. How you handle the steps in the employment relationship is essential to creating a strong defense in the event of such a legal action. Answer the questions on the sample *Checklist for a Termination Decision* on the CD that comes with this product before terminating an employee. It alerts you to the possible negative repercussions that could follow a termination. Should you determine that termination is in order, use the sample *Termination Checklist* on the CD that comes with this product to assist you in the process. For more information about the using the *Termination Checklist*, see "Obligations upon Termination" on page 170.

The Law Explained

There are several important exceptions to the at–will doctrine, including:

- An employee may not be terminated for discriminatory reasons (for example, race, sex, disability, age, or other protected classes);

- Employers who terminate employees with higher salaries as a cost cutting measure may be liable for age discrimination, if those terminated are mostly workers over the age of 40;

- If a precedent or policy has been set by the employer, a termination should not violate that precedent or policy;

- Employees may not be terminated in violation of established public policy or for retaliatory reasons. These include:

  - Exercising personal rights;

  - Whistleblowing (informing a state or federal agency of illegal activity of the employer);

  - Serving on a jury or attending court when subpoenaed as a witness; or

  - Cooperating in an official investigation against the employer.

- California's workers' compensation laws prohibit discrimination (including termination) against employees who file workers' compensation claims.

An employee's ability to collect punitive damage awards in contract–based wrongful termination lawsuits has been limited by the California Supreme Court. However, in some types of cases involving violations of public policy, discrimination or defamation, huge punitive damages continue to be awarded. Even where punitive damages are not available, employees can collect back pay for what often amounts to several years and, in some cases, front pay for loss of probable future income is available.

Policies

Employment policies and statements in employment advertisements or employee handbooks can cause you to lose the absolute right to terminate at–will. A poorly drafted policy creating a multi–step disciplinary procedure may be interpreted as preventing you from terminating an employee for a single act or rule violation. A stated policy of disciplining or terminating only for cause or just cause places an additional burden on you to prove a justifiable reason for your actions. Seniority systems modify the right to terminate at–will in layoff situations.

Practices

Notwithstanding clear statements in policy manuals and employee handbooks, your company's management can place limitations on your right to terminate at–will by employing practices that are inconsistent with your written words.

Example: If employees regularly remain employed despite exceeding the amount of sick leave provided for by your employee handbook, you may be liable for wrongful termination if a single employee is fired for that reason. Such practices may give rise to an implied contract of employment or not to terminate employment except under certain circumstances.

Contracts

An oral or written contract specifying that employment will continue for a specified period of time as long as stated performance requirements are met or that the employee will not be fired without good cause, modifies at–will employment. You would have the burden of proving the condition that justified termination or providing a legitimate business reason for terminating such an employee. If you do not provide such a reason, the employee may have a breach of contract claim.

Implied Contracts

An implied contract may be found to exist based on circumstances of employment, including long–term employment, good evaluations and raises. Under a California Supreme Court decision, courts must look to the "totality of the circumstances" to determine whether an implied contract exists. The critical factors include:

- The personnel policies or practices of the employer;

- The employee's length of service;

- Actions or communications by the employer that provide assurances of continued employment; and

- The practices of the particular industry.[1]

However an implied contract will not be inferred simply based on an employee's length of service, satisfactory performance and receipt of pay increases. Where the employer has an express at–will policy, an implied contract of employment will be found only if the employer has created, through words or conduct, a specific understanding that employment will be terminated only for good cause.[2]

---

1. *Foley v. Interactive Data Corp.*, 47 Cal.3d 654, (1998)
2. *Guz v. Bechtel National, Inc.*, 24 Cal. 4th 317 (2000)

Unions and Union Activity

Union contracts generally contain multi-step disciplinary procedures and complex grievance procedures making it more difficult to discipline or terminate employees. Federal and state laws prohibit employers from disciplining or terminating employees for having engaged in lawful activities on behalf of unions.

Laws

Certain activities are protected by the law and you may not terminate an employee for participating in such activities. The California Chamber's *2004 California Labor Law Digest* includes extensive discussion on these legal protections, including:

- Having wages garnished;
- Disclosing or refusing to disclose wages;
- Voluntary participating in alcohol or drug rehabilitation program;
- Refusing to authorize disclosure of medical information;
- Participating in jury duty;
- Political activity;
- Military service;
- Acting as volunteer firefighter;
- Refusing to do business with employer;
- Refusing to commit an illegal act;
- Taking time off to appear at a child's school regarding a suspension;
- Taking time off for a child's school or day care activities;
- Taking time off as a victim of domestic violence to obtain a restraining order, to receive care/counseling or to relocate;
- Maintaining privacy of arrest records that do not lead to convictions;
- Refusing to take polygraph test;
- Enrolling in an adult literacy program;
- Refusing to participate in abortions;
- Being considered for employment without regard to results of blood test for AIDS;
- Serving as election officer on election day;

- Health care workers reporting apparent victims of abuse or neglect as an exercise of statutory obligation, without suffering discharge or discipline; and

- Preventing an employee from disclosing information about a violation of law to a government or law enforcement agency.

Whistleblower Protection

New for 2004 You may not adopt or enforce any rule, regulation or policy preventing an employee from disclosing information to a government or law enforcement agency, where the employee has reasonable cause to believe that the information discloses a violation of state or federal statute, or a violation or noncompliance with a state or federal rule or regulation. The law also prohibits retaliation against an employee for disclosing information to a government or law enforcement agency, where the employee has reasonable cause to believe that the information discloses a violation of state or federal statute, or a violation or noncompliance with a state or federal rule or regulation. An employee who refuses to participate in an activity that would result in a violation of state or federal statute, or a violation or noncompliance with a state or federal rule or regulation is also protected from retaliation.

Constructive Discharge

An employee who resigns can nonetheless bring a claim for constructive discharge. This claim alleges that the employer has decided that, rather than terminating the employee, he/she will simply make conditions so intolerable that the employee resigns. A claim of constructive discharge can also be used by an employee who was given the "choice" of quitting rather than being fired.

In order to sustain a constructive discharge claim, an employee must show that the working conditions causing him/her to resign were sufficiently extraordinary and egregious that a reasonable person would be compelled to resign. In addition, the employee must have notified the employer of these conditions prior to resigning.[3]

Two situations that do not constitute constructive discharge are:

- Renegotiation of a compensation agreement does not create the intolerable working conditions necessary to sustain a constructive discharge claim;[4] and

- An employee's demotion.[5]

---

3. *Gibson v. Aro Corporation*, 32 Cal. App. 4th 1628 (1995); *Turner v. Anheuser–Busch, Inc.*, 7 Cal. 4th 1238 (1994)

4. *King v. AC&R Advertising*, 65 F.3d 764 (1995)

5. *Turner v. Anheuser–Busch, Inc.*, 7 Cal. 4th 1238 (1994)

What You Should Do

Your best defense against wrongful termination lawsuits is using the procedures discussed in this book, beginning with hiring the right employees, maintaining high standards of performance and engaging in appropriate disciplinary action. To avoid or defend against wrongful termination lawsuits, keep in mind the following as you move through the processes of recruitment through termination:

- **Document everything** — When faced with an angry former employee and a wrongful termination lawsuit, nothing is more helpful than a personnel file containing documentation showing that you properly:

  - Followed an established progressive discipline program;

  - Gave the employee honest performance evaluations;

  - Tracked the employee's attendance problem; and

  - Attempted to accommodate the employee's needs.

- **Don't use the term "probationary period"** — Also, avoid any type of introductory period if at all possible. Courts have construed the term "probationary period" to mean that once an employee has been employed for a certain amount of time, there is an implication that the employee has become "permanent" or achieved a status requiring good cause for termination. The better policy is simply to hire all employees on an at–will basis and avoid any type of introductory period;

- **Use caution when terminating protected class employees** — Think through the possibility of the appearance of a discriminatory motive before terminating any employee. This does not mean that you can never terminate a person in a protected class. It does mean that even if the intent to discriminate never crossed your mind, you could be faced with defending an expensive lawsuit because you didn't think through the possibilities first. When faced with the prospect of terminating an employee in a protected class, be sure you have all the documentation you need to show that the termination is based on legitimate, nondiscriminatory reasons; and

- **Train your managers and supervisors thoroughly** — No matter how much you know about avoiding a wrongful termination lawsuit, if your managers and supervisors do not follow your guidelines, you will be the one to pay the price. Take the time to ensure that they know how to handle problem employees, how to avoid sexual harassment in the workplace and how to ensure that implied contracts of employment are not created.

 Use the sample *Checklist for a Termination Decision* on the CD that comes with this product to evaluate your termination decision.

For more information, see the California Chamber's *2004 **California Labor Law Digest***, which devotes an entire chapter to the subject of employee termination and employment at–will.

Multi–Step (Progressive) Discipline

Nothing in the law dictates how you maintain order in your company, but many companies have adopted a process for doing so based on a series of increasingly serious actions. A multi–step (progressive) discipline program usually consists of a series of steps ranging from a verbal warning to termination. Whatever program you choose to implement, keep in mind that it is important for any progressive discipline program to specify that management has full discretion at all times to determine the appropriate level of discipline for a given offense, regardless of the "normal" procedure and to take any action, including immediate termination.

The Law Explained

Progressive discipline is not required by law, but you need to make clear to your employees what conduct is expected and what is prohibited. When the conduct of an employee violates one of these standards, employee discipline of some sort is required. Accurate and consistent documentation of employee discipline is essential to running an efficient business, avoiding unwarranted unemployment insurance claims and defending your company against wrongful termination lawsuits.

What You Should Do

A progressive discipline program usually consists of a series of steps ranging from a verbal warning to termination. A typical program consists of a verbal warning, one or two written warnings, probation or suspension and finally termination. Of course, you may set up your progressive discipline program in any way you like, depending on the needs of your workplace.

Employers often divide violations into categories, differentiating behavioral issues from performance issues. Attendance problems are also usually treated as a distinct matter, particularly where an employer has an absenteeism control policy that tracks days off work (see "Attendance Control" on page 168). An employee is warned verbally on the first occasion of each type of infraction. Therefore, a violation of the attendance policy on Monday would give rise to a verbal warning and violation of a safety rule on Wednesday also would receive a verbal warning. Both verbal warnings should, of course, be documented. However, if an employee's rule violation continues, you would move forward to a written warning, if you reserved the right to apply whatever discipline is deemed appropriate in a given situation. Be sure that you apply the progressive discipline program uniformly and reserve exceptions for times when they are truly necessary for the health and safety of employees, or for flagrant violations of important rules.

Investigating Misconduct

Before disciplining an employee, conduct a thorough investigation so the action you take is justifiable. California courts require you to reach reasonable conclusions from an adequate, impartial investigation. You can best defend claims of wrongful termination if the investigation meets that standard. At a minimum, promptly investigate all reasonable sources of information and give the employee notice of the allegation and an opportunity to respond. If you act reasonably based on adequate information, courts will generally uphold your action even if they disagree with the result. Let the full extent of the investigation be determined by the seriousness of the incident and extent of the potential penalty.

New for 2004 The U.S. Supreme Court has ruled that union represented employees have the right, upon their request, to have a union representative present during any investigatory interview that the employee believes may result in discipline.[6] The National Labor Relations Board has ruled that this right does not apply to non-union employees who request assistance during an investigatory interview.[7]

When you learn of employee misconduct, respond quickly. In serious cases, especially those involving violent or illegal activity or sexual harassment, seek employment law counsel to provide risk assessment and direction before beginning the investigation. You can then assess the need for and scope of an investigation by considering the following:

- What facts will be needed to support the decision making process?

- How can you develop a thorough record on which to base an opinion?

- What steps are needed to protect the confidentiality of your investigation?

- What policies, rules or criminal laws may have been violated?

- If criminal activity has occurred, do you want or are you obligated to inform appropriate authorities?

- What steps need be taken to limit the company's liability?

---

6. *NLRB v. Weinsarten,* 420 U.S. 251, (1975)

7. *IBM Corp.,* 341 NLRB No. 148, (June 15, 2004)

- How can you stop a potential problem from expanding? and

- What is the appropriate disciplinary action if the alleged facts are true?

Select an appropriate investigator, someone who is not involved in the situation and can conduct a full, fair and objective investigation. Be sure that the person selected is a good listener who can obtain the necessary information, assess the credibility of the persons interviewed and write a factual report of findings. The investigator should be a person who is known to be fair, knows the policies and procedures and would be credible to a judge or jury if litigation occurs. The investigation must identify the following:

- What happened?

- When did it happen?

- Where did it happen?

- Who was involved in the incident and who witnessed it?

- Why did it happen?

The following actions can make your investigation more productive:

- Prepare a strategy by creating an investigation plan and then begin by meeting with all parties who have knowledge of the incident;

- Create an outline of questions for witnesses, identifying key areas that need to be investigated and relevant documents that may provide supporting evidence. You want to know the whole story, including facts that may not ultimately support your conclusions;

- Design the interviews to obtain and determine the important facts. All parties and witnesses should be interviewed separately and individually. You may need to question witnesses more than once; and

- On all but the simplest issues, take written statements and have them signed and dated.

Keep notes and the investigation report separate from personnel files and secure them along with any evidence. Your notes and the investigation report may be subject to subpoena should litigation follow.

The investigation report should be an impartial recitation of the facts and evidence. Include a summary of the witnesses interviewed and an analysis based on the information obtained during the investigation. Draw conclusions based on the investigation only. Keep in mind that a reviewing court will look at whether or not you had a rational good faith basis for making your decision. When making a decision based on the investigation report, consider the following:

- **Notice of rules and expectations** — Were the rules clear and communicated so the employee has knowledge of expectations and the possible or probable disciplinary consequences of the employee's conduct? Exceptions may be made for serious misconduct that all employees are expected to know are punishable without prior warning, such as fighting, stealing or insubordination;

- **Reasonableness of rule or order** — Was the rule or order reasonably related to the orderly, efficient and safe operation of the business and to performance that you might properly expect of the employee? An employee may have justification for disobeying a rule or order or even legal protection for doing so.

Example: An employee is protected from retaliation where the employee believes the order would seriously and immediately jeopardize his/her personal safety and/or integrity, or violate a federal or state law, regulation or rule.

- **Sufficiency of investigation** — Did you investigate before imposing discipline and was the investigation fair and objective? Where immediate action is required, put the employee on leave pending the outcome of the investigation, with the understanding that he/she will be restored to his/her job if found not guilty;

- **Adequacy of proof** — Did the investigation produce substantial evidence or proof that the employee is guilty as charged?

- **Equality of treatment** — Have rules, orders and penalties been applied evenly and without discrimination? What kinds of corrective action have been taken within your department for similar offenses? If enforcement has been lax, management cannot suddenly reverse its course and start enforcing policies without first warning employees of its intent; and

- **Appropriateness of penalty** — Is the discipline reasonably related to the seriousness of the offense and the employee's past record? Did you consider any mitigating or aggravating circumstances, such as the employee's prior performance evaluations, longevity and documented disciplinary actions?

> Consult legal counsel when the incident involves a case of unlawful harassment, sexual or otherwise. Additional information and strategies may be found in the California Chamber's *2004 California Labor Law Digest* and its companion publication, *Managing to Avoid Sexual Harassment*.

Documenting Disciplinary Actions

The most common mistake made by employers when enforcing a discipline program is the failure to put absolutely everything in writing. Although it may seem odd that a verbal warning is the subject of a written document, it is essential to create a written record of such a warning and to retain it in the employee's personnel file. When faced with an unemployment insurance claim or a wrongful termination lawsuit, without documentation to show that a verbal warning was given, you may have a difficult time proving the employee did in fact receive such a warning.

For simplicity and consistency, use the same format to document all employee discipline. The *Employee Warning* form may be used for a verbal or written warning, probation and suspension. The final step, termination, requires you to follow the process outlined in "Obligations upon Termination" on page 170.

New for 2004 Disciplinary action should include a face–to–face private meeting with the employee. Never engage in a disciplinary action in a non–private setting. Subjecting an employee to disciplinary action in the presence of others has been held by a California court to violate the employee's constitutional right to privacy. [8]

Be well prepared for the meeting, having gathered all the facts necessary to support the action to be taken. Otherwise, the employee may sense your lack of preparedness and use the opportunity to challenge the validity of the action. Inform the employee of all the facts and ask him/her to sign written warnings that will go into his/her personnel file. To be the most useful tool, employee warnings should focus not only on the nature of the infraction, but on the steps the employee must take to correct his/her conduct and the consequences of failing to do so. Include these steps on the written record of the warning so that they can be referred to easily if the employee fails to improve.

Encourage the employee to fill in the "Employee Response" section, either to suggest ways to improve or to document his/her view of the incident. There is no need to have the employee sign the written record of a verbal warning, as this simply is your documentation that you have given a verbal warning. Ask the employee to sign all other types of disciplinary warnings and then keep them in the employee's personnel file.

Because many employees take exception to being reprimanded, be sure to emphasize to your employee that his/her signature is not necessarily an admission of wrongdoing, but simply an acknowledgment that he/she has received a warning. If an employee will not sign the written record, make a note of that fact on the warning, have another manager witness the employee's refusal to sign, if possible and then file the record in the personnel file. Under California law, the employee is entitled to a copy of the warning record if he/she has signed it.

 For more information, review the sample *Employee Warning* on the CD that comes with this product.

---

8. *Operating Engineers Local 3 v. Johnson*, 110 Cal. App. 4th 180 (Cal. App., 1st Dist., 2003)

Attendance Control

Attendance and tardiness are two of the most frequent and difficult to discipline behavioral. Supervisors may often be faced with making judgments about the relative justification for absences or tardiness presented by different employees. Often, the employee's longevity and general performance records influence the supervisor's perception of the acceptability of the excuse. For this reason, many companies have adopted objective measures that define how much absenteeism and how many incidents of tardiness are acceptable in a given time period. Although some subjectivity may still determine whether a particular incident should be charged against the employee, using objective measures that help ensure your attendance control policy is applied uniformly.

The Law Explained

There are no legal standards that say how much absenteeism or tardiness an employer must endure before taking disciplinary action. There are, however, some legal constraints as to what incidents can be counted against an employee. Absences that are protected by law, including the federal Family medical Leave Act (FMLA), the California Family Rights Act (CFRA), the California Pregnancy Disability Leave (PDL) and California "kin care" cannot be charged against an employee's attendance record. Other reasons for absence also are protected by state law. Finally, failure to administer attendance standards in an equal manner may result in a discrimination or retaliation claim, even if you are using an apparently objective system.

There are special rules for deducting from an exempt employee's salary, including deductions for absenteeism. To ensure your exempt employees remain exempt (and therefore not subject to overtime and other wage requirements), follow these special rules carefully. Also, you may not deduct from wages of a non–exempt employee due to tardiness any amount in excess of the amount that the employee would have earned during the time actually missed. However, if the loss of time is less than 30 minutes, one–half hour of wages may be deducted, but you may not put the employee to work during that half–hour period. The California Chamber's *2004 California Labor Law Digest* and the companion book in this series, *Managing Leaves of Absence in California*, will help you stay out of trouble while controlling absenteeism. You may order these products by calling the California Chamber at (800) 331–8877 or by visiting our online store at *http://www.calchamberstore.com*.

What You Should Do

The knowledge that you keep detailed attendance records may be enough to deter some employee abuse of sick time and vacation policies. Review an employee's attendance records when you are preparing his/her performance evaluation. Depending on the size and organization of your company, attendance records may be kept by your personnel department staff, bookkeeper, office manager, supervisors, or any other designated employee. Establish a system that makes sense for your company and stick to it.

Monitor attendance daily for accuracy. Attendance records for all employees are most easily kept in a single location, such as a binder, where they can be updated daily. At the end of each year, place a copy of each employee's annual attendance record in his/her personnel file and begin a new form. Attendance also needs to be reported to whoever handles your payroll, as deductions need to be made for time not worked.

 For more information, review the sample *Attendance Record* and sample *Attendance Record Summary* on the CD that comes with this product.

Exit Interviews

Many employers choose not to take advantage of the opportunity to conduct exit interviews because one that is completed by a hostile employee can create documentation that could be damaging in a lawsuit or claim for unemployment insurance (UI) benefits. On the other hand, an exit interview could provide information that an employee is leaving your company for a substantially better job. This information may be significant for you because UI benefits paid to an employee who leave one job for a substantially better one and who later becomes eligible for UI, are not chargeable to the account of the previous employer (you). This situation might occur if the former employee lost the new job or had his/her hours reduced by the new employer.

The Law Explained

An exit interview is not required by law. It is simply a chance for you to learn from a departing employee his/her thoughts about employment with your company.

What You Should Do

The sample *Exit Interview* on the CD that comes with this product includes a series of questions that would indicate whether an employee is leaving for a substantially better job. Conduct an exit interview on the final day of employment, or allow the employee to take the form home and return it by mail. If completed by mail, provide the employee with a postage-paid return envelope marked "confidential" and addressed to the person in your company authorized to receive the completed exit interview. You may fill in the employee's answers if the exit interview is conducted orally. However, you are more likely to receive candid answers if an employee is allowed to fill out the exit interview form himself/herself. Keep the exit interview in the employee's personnel file.

Obligations upon Termination

There are issues you must consider and requirements you must fulfill any time the employment relationship is terminated. Use the sample *Termination Checklist* on the CD that comes with this product to identify the required and recommended forms you should fill out during the termination process.

The Law Explained

Prior to advising an employee of his/her termination, you must be prepared to pay all amounts due.

If the separation is a voluntary termination (employee-initiated resignation or retirement), a final paycheck must be issued within 72 hours of the final date of employment, or on the last day of employment if more than 72 hours notice was given. If the separation is an involuntary termination (employer-initiated discharges or layoff with no specified date of rehire), all wages and accrued vacation earned but unpaid are due and payable on the last day of work.

Overtime Pay

Use the following information to properly compute overtime pay earned during the final pay period.

Time-and-one-half is required for:

- Any work over eight hours in a single day;
- The first eight hours on the seventh consecutive day worked in a single workweek; and
- Work beyond 40 straight-time hours in a single workweek.

Double time is required for:

- Any work over 12 hours in a day;

Helping California Business Do Business®

- Any hours beyond eight on the seventh consecutive day worked in a single workweek; and

- Any hours beyond eight on the seventh consecutive day worked in a single workweek. If, for example, the workweek is defined as Sunday through Saturday, the seventh day rule will apply only on the seventh day of that specifically defined workweek.

Commissions on monies you have not yet received may be paid out after the time the final paycheck is due to an employee, if commissions are not normally earned until you have received payment. For example, if an employee has made a sale but the customer has not yet paid the invoice, no payment is due the employee for that sale until you receives payment from the customer.

 See "Wage Deductions for Unreturned Property" in Chapter 5, page 127, for information about deductions for unreturned employer property.

For more information about California's wage and hour laws, refer to the California Chamber's *2004 California Labor Law Digest*.

What You Should Do

Once a decision has been made to discharge an employee or a notice of voluntary termination is received, collect all timecards and documentation regarding the employee's unpaid work period, outstanding advances and expenses. Notify the person responsible for issuing the final paycheck of the time constraints. Use the *Final Paycheck Worksheet* on the CD that comes with this product to calculate and, if applicable, prorate the amount of time actually worked, through the final day of work. Include regular hours, overtime and paid holidays that fall in this period, plus any accrued paid vacation.

Consider any other benefits that may be due to the employee, such as accrued and payable sick leave (if paid to the employee under your employment policies), severance pay, expenses advanced by the employee on behalf of you, etc.

After determining the amount due to the employee, make the proper calculations for any deductions, such as:

- Federal, state and local income taxes;

- Social Security;

- Medicare;

- State unemployment insurance;

- State disability insurance (SDI);

- Life insurance;

- Health insurance;

- Long–term disability; and

- Miscellaneous items, such as advances; parking, etc.

In addition to the *Final Paycheck Worksheet*, use the *Final Paycheck Acknowledgement* form, also located on the CD that comes with this product, to document the employee's receipt of his/her final paycheck. Having employees sign that they have received the final paycheck allows you to document that the last paycheck deadline was met, as required. It also gives you an opportunity to clarify with the employee that proper payment was received. Neither of the forms is required, but they are good business documentation.

Employee Notices

You are required to provide terminating employees, whether they resign or are discharged, with certain notices. The following discussion about these notices will assist you in identifying, using and providing the appropriate notices.

Notice to Employee as to Change in Relationship (Termination Notice)

When an employee is involuntarily terminated, whether because of a layoff, discharge or change in relationship to independent contractor, you must give the employee written notice of the change in relationship.

The Law Explained

You must give immediate written notice to an employee for a discharge, layoff, or leave of absence.[9] Give this notice to your employee no later than the effective date of the termination. The notice must contain, at a minimum, the:

- Name of the employer;

- Name of the employee;

- Social Security number (SSN) of the employee;

---

9. Section 1089 of the California Unemployment Insurance Code

- Reason for the change: whether the action was a discharge, layoff, leave of absence, or a change in status from employee to independent contractor; and

- Date of the action.

You are not required to give the notice to an employee who voluntarily quits, although you may want to do so. Should the employee apply for UI benefits, you can refer to the termination notice to verify the reason for separation. If the employee left your company voluntarily without good cause, but tries to collect UI benefits, you can use the notice to protest an improper UI claim. A successful appeal can prevent improper assessment against your company's UI account and save your company thousands of dollars.

There is no required, official government notice for you to use. You can provide written notice by:

- Drafting a letter;

- Creating a notice of your own design; or

- Using the sample *Notice to Employee as to Change in Relationship* on the CD that comes with this product.

What You Should Do

A supervisor or human resource specialist should complete the notice. The person completing the form should state/choose the reason for the separation carefully and communicate it to the employee. An improperly reported reason could be costly for your company. Although employers cannot misrepresent the facts of the termination to avoid paying UI benefits, benefits should not be paid to those who are ineligible according to the law.

The notice must include:

- The name of the employer;

- The name of the employee;

- Social Security number of the employee;

- Indication that the action was a discharge, layoff, leave of absence, or a change in status; and

- The date of the action.

Employers are often hesitant to terminate an employee because they do not want to pay UI benefits. So it's important for you to understand when an employee is eligible for UI benefits and what you can do to prepare the documentation necessary to fight a claim that should be denied. See Chapter 9, "Managing Unemployment Compensation" for more information about UI, including eligibility issues and responding to a claim for benefits.

Use the sample *Notice to Employee as to Change in Relationship* to meet EDD requirements and protest UI claims by an ineligible employee. Employers who document a specific reason for discharge (such as poor attendance or performance) also may use this form to help defend against employee allegations of wrongful or discriminatory discharge. The *Notice* provides check boxes for you to choose the reason the employment status has changed. The specified reasons correspond with the factors considered by the EDD in determining the eligibility of an applicant for UI benefits. This form is valuable documentation should you choose to contest a claim for such benefits. Following are the reasons for termination listed on the *Notice*:

- **Voluntary quit** — which mean the employee has chosen to leave his/her job voluntarily. Such a person would be ineligible for UI compensation unless he/she can establish good cause attributed to the employer, or compelling personal reasons;

  An employee may quit a job and still be eligible for UI when good cause is a substantial motivating factor in causing the claimant to leave work. The motivating factor may or may not be work–connected; must be real, substantial and compelling; and must be something that would cause a reasonable person genuinely desirous of retaining employment to leave work under the same circumstances;

- **Layoff** — which means that available work ends either temporarily or permanently through no fault of the employee. This claimant most likely would be eligible for UI benefits;

- **Leaves of absence** — which usually occur for reasons of health, pregnancy, discipline or a sabbatical offered by the employer. This claimant may be eligible to collect UI benefits;

- **Discharge** — which means the employer has good cause to discharge an employee within the parameters of company policy or union agreement, but requires that the employer establish misconduct to avoid paying UI benefits;

- **Refusal to accept available work** — which means the employee has refused to perform work that is:

  - Appropriate to the individual's health, safety, morals and physical condition;

  - Consistent with the individual's prior experience and earnings; and

  - A reasonable distance from the individual's residence.

  This claimant most likely would be ineligible to collect UI benefits.

- **Change in status** — which means that the employee–employer relationship is being terminated, but that you may choose to hire this person as an independent contractor. For more information about determining independent contractor status, see "Employing Independent Contractors" in Chapter 2, page 37.

Give the completed termination notice to the employee. Although not required by law, request the employee's signature acknowledging receipt of the termination notice. EDD does not require you to submit a copy of the termination notice. Retain a copy in the employee's personnel record.

"For Your Benefit" Pamphlet (Form DE 2320)

The *For Your Benefit (Form 2320)* pamphlet was created by EDD to explain employees' rights to both unemployment insurance (UI) and state disability insurance (SDI).

The Law Explained

Whether an employee is discharged or voluntarily quits, you must give the terminating employee written notice of his/her UI benefit rights by providing the sample *For Your Benefit (Form 2320)* pamphlet. This notice must be given no later than the effective date of the termination.

What You Should Do

This pamphlet requires no preparation. Simply give a copy to the terminating employee.

The pamphlet is available through the California Chamber or EDD. You may order it from the California Chamber by calling (800) 331-8877 or from EDD by mailing or faxing the *Requisition for EDD Forms*. You also may order the pamphlet directly on EDD's website at ***http://www.edd.ca.gov/taxrep/taxordn2.htm***.

For more information, refer to EDD's *California Employer's Guide (DE 44)* "Notices and Pamphlets for Employees" section. You also may order the *DE 44* using EDD's *Requisition for EDD Forms*.

Notice of COBRA Rights

Notifying employees of their COBRA rights provides terminated employees with information necessary to continue coverage under your group health, dental and vision insurance plans.

The Law Explained

Any employer with a group insurance plan who has 20 or more employees must give notice of Consolidated Omnibus Budget Reconciliation Act of 1985 (COBRA) rights, which entitles "qualified beneficiaries" to continued benefits under the group insurance plan. For more information, see "Who's a Qualified Beneficiary?" on page 177. For purposes of COBRA, the 20 employee minimum includes all full–time and part–time employees, regardless of whether all employees participate in the group insurance plan. An employer is considered as having normally employed fewer than 20 employees during a calendar year if it had fewer than 20 employees on at least 50% of its typical business days that year. If you are part of a multi–employer plan, you should check with your insurance agent to determine COBRA applicability. If you have fewer than 20 employees, see "Cal–COBRA Notice to Carrier" on page 179.

Notice of COBRA rights must be given to a qualified beneficiary within 14 days of the time you are notified of a qualifying event. For more information, see "What's a Qualifying Event?" on page 177. This duty is imposed on the plan administrator, who usually is the employer, unless another plan administrator is specifically designated.

The most common situations in which notice of COBRA rights must be given are when covered employees are terminated (other than for gross misconduct) or when employees' hours are reduced such that they are no longer eligible to participate in the group health plan. For more information, see "Who's a Covered Employee?" on page 177. Keep in mind that termination includes resignations, layoffs, job abandonment, etc. Each of the other qualifying events listed in "What's a Qualifying Event?" on page 177, also triggers your obligation to provide notice of COBRA rights.

You must offer COBRA coverage to qualified beneficiaries who would lose coverage under the your group health insurance plan due to certain "qualifying events." The qualified beneficiary usually is required to pay the cost of the continued health coverage. You may charge the qualified beneficiary a two percent administrative fee. For more information, see "What's a Qualifying Event?" on page 177.

 For more information, review the sample *COBRA Election Form (California), COBRA Election Form (Outside California)* and sample *Acknowledgement of Receipt of Notification of COBRA Rights* on the CD that comes with this product.

Who's a Covered Employee?

A covered employee is any individual who was provided coverage under a group health plan as a result of performing services for the employer.

Who's a Qualified Beneficiary?

A qualified beneficiary is a/an:

- Covered employee whose employment is terminated, either voluntarily or involuntarily, except one who is terminated for gross misconduct;

- Employee whose hours of work are reduced to a level that would preclude his/her from coverage under the employer's plan;

- Covered spouse and dependent children of the covered employee; and

- Children born to or placed for adoption with a covered employee during the COBRA continuation period.

What's a Qualifying Event?

A qualifying event under COBRA is one which would otherwise result in the loss of coverage by a qualified beneficiary. Under COBRA, six events can be qualifying events if they result in loss of coverage. The following table details these six events and the maximum length of coverage they trigger.

Table 19. Qualifying Events

Qualifying event	Maximum length of coverage
Death of the covered employee	36 months
Termination (other than for reasons such as employee's gross misconduct), or reduction of hours of the covered employee's employment	18 months
Divorce or legal separation of the covered employee from the employee's spouse	36 months
The covered employee becomes entitled to benefits under Medicare	36 months
The dependent child ceases to be a dependent child under the generally applicable requirements of the plan	36 months
An employer's bankruptcy, but only as it relates to health care coverage for retirees and their dependents	36 months

A 2002 amendment to the Cal–COBRA law extends the maximum coverage to 36 months for all California employees and beneficiaries whose continuation coverage began on or after January 1, 2003.

Reducing or Eliminating Benefits

You cannot reduce or eliminate health coverage in anticipation of a qualifying event. If you do so, the qualified beneficiary may be entitled to the benefit that would otherwise be lost. An across–the–board reduction or elimination of benefits may be seen as being done in anticipation of a qualifying event. In that situation, you might be required to make coverage available where there is a qualifying event. To counter such a position, when reducing or eliminating health coverage benefits, carefully document that such an event was not meant to circumvent COBRA.

Extending COBRA for Retirees

California law requires that California employers extend COBRA coverage to retirees and their spouses for an additional five years after retirement. The law requires that certain retirees and their spouses be allowed to continue coverage by arrangement directly with their insurers when the employee worked at least five years before the termination with the same employer and was at least 60 years old at the time of termination. If you have an employee entitled to the extended state coverage, you may wish to seek legal counsel.

Medical Spending Accounts

Under IRS regulations, medical spending accounts (funded by pre–tax employee contributions) generally are excluded from COBRA, provided that such an account, under a flexible benefit/cafeteria plan, provides for changes in the election because of the COBRA–qualifying event. This means that the plan participant can revoke his/her cafeteria plan election to stop/change pretax deductions. If termination of employment is the qualifying event, an employee typically has no further wages from which payment could be deducted. However, if the qualifying event is a dependent losing dependent status or an employee reducing his/her hours, the change can allow potentially for the employee to pay for COBRA coverage on a pre–tax basis.

What You Should Do

You fill out the top of the *COBRA Election Form* before mailing or giving it to the qualified beneficiary. The qualified beneficiary fills out the bottom portion acknowledging that he/she has received the notice with his/her signature and returns it to you. If you are sending the notification by mail, be sure to send it certified mail so that you will receive a return receipt. File the signed acknowledgment or return receipt in the employee's personnel file as proof that proper COBRA notification was given.

 The Internal Revenue Service (IRS) has prepared a document designed to help *employees* who may be confused about whether to elect COBRA coverage since the passage of HIPAA health insurance portability provisions. Called *IRS Notice 98-12*, employers are not required to provide this document, but it may help employees who have a qualifying event make informed decisions about electing COBRA coverage. *IRS Notice 98-12* is available on the IRS website at ***http://www.irs.ustreas.gov/prod/news/index.html***.

COBRA is a very complex area of the law. The California Chamber's ***2004 California Labor Law Digest*** has a full chapter detailing COBRA requirements and coverage. To purchase a copy of the book, call (800) 331–8877, or visit the California Chamber store at ***http://www.calchamberstore.com***.

The IRS has COBRA and HIPAA resources available for employers or plan administrators responsible for plan activities at (202) 622–6080.

You also may obtain more information by contacting the U.S. Department of Labor's (DOL):
Pension and Welfare Benefits Administration
Room N5625
U.S. Department of Labor
200 Constitution Avenue NW
Washington, DC 20210
(202) 219–8776

Cal–COBRA Notice to Carrier

The Cal–COBRA law was originally passed to provide continuation of health benefits for terminated employees of employers who were too small to be covered by federal COBRA. Subsequently, the Cal–COBRA law was amended to enhance federal COBRA rights by extending the coverage continuation period to 36 months for all California residents.

The Law Explained

Group health and disability carriers must provide COBRA–like insurance continuation benefits for employers of two to 19 employees who offer health/disability insurance.

Cal–COBRA requires insurance carriers to provide continuation of benefits if the employee or a qualified beneficiary loses coverage as a result of a qualifying event (see "Who's a Qualified Beneficiary?" on page 177). Qualifying events that entitle employees/beneficiaries to coverage are:

- The death of the covered employee or subscriber;

- The termination or reduction of hours of the covered employee's or subscriber's employment (termination for gross misconduct does not constitute a qualifying event);

- Divorce or legal separation of the covered employee's spouse;

- Loss of dependent status by a dependent enrolled in the group benefit plan; and

- With respect to a dependent only, the covered employee's or subscriber's eligibility for coverage under Medicare.

You must notify your group health/disability insurers of any employee or qualified beneficiary who will lose coverage as a result of a termination or reduction in hours, within 31 days of the qualifying event. Employees and qualified beneficiaries must provide notice to the insurer within 60 days of any of the other listed qualifying events in order to be eligible for Cal–COBRA.

 For more information, review the sample *Cal-COBRA - Notice to Carrier* on the CD that comes with this product.

What You Should Do

Complete the *Cal-COBRA - Notice to Carrier* when an employee or qualified beneficiary becomes subject to Cal–COBRA because of a termination or reduction in hours. Your carrier must be notified within 31 days of the qualifying event.

Mail the original notice to your insurance carrier. Keep a copy in the employee's personnel file as proof that the insurer was notified within the required time period.

Because the burden of Cal–COBRA falls mainly on your insurance carrier, contact your carrier with any questions you may have about this law.

HIPAA Certificate

The Health Insurance Portability and Accountability Act of 1996 (HIPAA) is a broad federal statute enacted to provide, among other things, better continuity of health insurance coverage for people who change employment, or who otherwise lose employer-sponsored health coverage.

The Law Explained

All employers who offer health insurance must provide employees who lose their rights to employer–sponsored health plan coverage with a *Certificate of Group Health Plan Coverage*. This situation normally occurs upon termination of employment or termination of COBRA or Cal–COBRA coverage. The certificate is required by the federal HIPAA, which limits the extent to which group health plans may subject new employees to pre–existing condition limitations.

You must provide the certificate within 14 days if the employee is eligible for COBRA, otherwise within a reasonable time (not defined by the HIPAA regulations). If an individual has elected COBRA coverage, provide the certificate within a reasonable time after the COBRA coverage ends, even though a certificate has already been provided at the time the individual became eligible for COBRA.

 For more information, review the sample *Certificate of Group Health Plan Coverage* on the CD that comes with this product.

What You Should Do

You complete the certificate and send it to the employee by first–class or registered mail. Dependents are entitled to their own certificates if their insurance information is not identical to that of the employee's. Keep a copy of all certificates issued in the employee's personnel file.

For more information about this complex federal law, see the California Chamber's **2004 *California Labor Law Digest*.**

Health Insurance Premium Payment Program (HIPP)

California's Medi-Cal program includes coverage for eligible persons who lose their employment-based health insurance.

The Law Explained

All employers who provide health insurance for their employees must notify employees who are terminated or who voluntarily quit of the availability of continued health insurance coverage through California's Medi-Cal program. This coverage is available at the state's expense under certain conditions. The California Department of Health Services may continue payment of health insurance premiums for certain persons losing employment who are eligible for Medi-Cal and have a high cost medical condition.

The *HIPPA Notice* requirements to terminating employees is in addition to the notification required by COBRA. For more information about COBRA, see "Notice of COBRA Rights" on page 176.

For more information, review the sample *HIPPA Notice (English)* and sample *HIPPA Notice (Spanish)* on the CD that comes with this product.

What You Should Do

The form is simply for the employee's information and does not need to be filled out. Give a copy of the form to each employee who is terminated or voluntarily resigns. Use the *Termination Checklist* on the CD that comes with this product to document that you gave the *HIPPA Notice* to the employee at termination.

You may obtain more information by contacting the California Department of Health Services at:

Department of Health Services
Third Party Liability Branch
Health Insurance Section
714/744 P Street
P.O. Box 1287
Sacramento, CA 95812-1287
(916) 323-9697

What Forms and Checklists Do I Use to Discipline and Terminate Employees?

The following table describes forms and checklists associated with disciplining and terminating employees.

You can find these forms on the CD that comes with this product.

Table 20. Required Forms and Checklists

Form/Checklist Name	What do I use it for?	When do I use it?	Who fills it out?	Where does it go?
Acknowledgement of Receipt of Notification of COBRA Rights	Required for all types of separation if your insurance plan has 20 or more participants	Within 14 days of the time you are notified of a qualifying event	Employee signs the notice	Send a notice via certified mail to the employee and spouse.
Cal-COBRA - Notice to Carrier	Required for all types of separation if your insurance plan has two to 19 participants	Within 31 days of the time of the qualifying events of either separation or reduction in hours	You do	Send the original form to insurance carrier within 31 days of the qualifying event. Keep a copy of the form in your personnel records.
Certificate of Group Health Plan Coverage	Required for all types of separation if you have an insurance plan	Within 14 days if the employee is eligible for COBRA, or otherwise within "reasonable" time	You do	Send the original certificate to employee by first class or registered mail. Dependents may need their own certificates. Keep a copy of the certificate in your personnel records.

Table 20. Required Forms and Checklists

Form/Checklist Name	What do I use it for?	When do I use it?	Who fills it out?	Where does it go?
COBRA Election Form (California)	Required for all types of separation if your insurance plan has 20 or more participants	Within 14 days of a qualifying event affecting a California resident	You fill out the required information The qualified beneficiary fills out the bottom of the election	Completed notice signed by the employee should be filed in your personnel records, along with the return receipt, if applicable. Keep a record of the date sent and the address to which it was sent.
COBRA Election Form (Outside California)	Required for all types of separation if your insurance plan has 20 or more participants	Within 14 days of a qualifying event affecting a non-California resident	You fill out the required information The qualified beneficiary fills out the bottom of the election	Completed notice signed by the employee should be filed in your personnel records, along with the return receipt, if applicable. Keep a record of the date sent and the address to which it was sent.
For Your Benefit (Form DE 2320)	Required for all types of separation	Immediately	Give a copy to the employee	Use the *Termination Checklist* to document that the form was given to the employee at separation.

Table 20. Required Forms and Checklists

Form/Checklist Name	What do I use it for?	When do I use it?	Who fills it out?	Where does it go?
HIPPA Notice (English) or *HIPPA Notice (Spanish)*	Required for all types of separation	Immediately	Give a copy to the employee	Use the *Termination Checklist* to document that the form was given to the employee at separation.
Notice to Employee as to Change in Relationship	Required for: • Discharge; • Layoff; and • Leave of absence. Recommended for *all* types of separation Written notice must be provided by: • Letter; • Employer's own form; or • The form discussed here.	In your preparations to terminate an employee	You do. Employee's signature should be requested but is not required by law.	Give a copy of the form to the employee. Keep a copy of the form in the employee's personnel records.

Table 21. Recommended Forms and Checklists

Form/Checklist Name	What do I use it for?	When do I use it?	Who fills it out?	Where does it go?
Attendance Record	To record each employee's absences	Daily, when an absence occurs	You do	Keep in employee's personnel file
Attendance Record Summary	To summarize past year's attendance for each employee	Year-end	You do	Keep in employee's personnel file
Checklist for a Termination Decision	Recommended for *all* types of separation	Before deciding to terminate an employee	You consider the questions	NA
Employee Warning	To document disciplinary actions	Fill out after investigating incident and before discussing discipline with employee	You do	Keep in employee's personnel file
Exit Interview	Recommended for *all* types of separation	On the final day of the employment, or ask the employee to return a paper form by mail	Employee should fill in answers unless interview is conducted orally, in which case, the employer may fill in the employee's answers	Keep the exit interview in your personnel records.
Final Paycheck Acknowledgement	To advise employee of final paycheck details and get acknowledgment of receipt by employee	Any termination	You do then it is signed by employee	Keep in employee's personnel file

Table 21. Recommended Forms and Checklists

Form/Checklist Name	What do I use it for?	When do I use it?	Who fills it out?	Where does it go?
Final Paycheck Worksheet	To compute final pay	Any termination	You do	Keep in employee's personnel file
Termination Checklist	Recommended for *all* types of separation	During the separation process	Employer keeps track of termination paperwork	Keep the checklist in your personnel records.

Chapter 9

Managing Unemployment Compensation

Even assuming that there is no challenge made to the decision to terminate an employee, the last day worked doesn't end your activities. You may receive a claim for unemployment compensation from your former employee.

The reason an individual is out of work can affect his/her eligibility for benefits. A person who is laid off is out of work through no fault of his/her own and is therefore eligible for benefits. A person who voluntarily quits or is terminated will be scheduled for a telephone interview with EDD because there is a separation issue that must be resolved. The EDD interviewer obtains and documents information about the separation from you and your former employee and decides, according to law and regulations, if the former employee is eligible to collect benefits. The EDD mails a notice to the claimant who is not eligible for benefits and mails a notice to you, if you responded in a timely fashion to the notice of claim filed. The notice advises you about whether the claimant is eligible and whether the your account is being charged for benefits paid to the former employee. Either party can disagree with an unfavorable decision and file an appeal.

The Law Explained

To be eligible for UI benefits, claimants must:

- Have made a claim for benefits in accordance with the regulations;

- Be unemployed through no fault of his or her own;

- Have earned at least $1,300 in one quarter or have high–quarter wages of $900 and total four quarter base–period earnings of 1.25 times that amount;

- Be available and able to work;

- Be actively looking for work; and

- Have registered for work and conducted a search for suitable work as directed.

There is a one-week waiting period after eligibility is established and before UI benefits are paid.

Claimants are found ineligible for unemployment benefits if they are out of work for one of the following reasons:

- Voluntary quit without good cause;

- Discharge for misconduct; or

- Refusal to perform suitable work.

Good cause for an employee voluntarily leaving work occurs when a substantial motivating factor causes the claimant to leave work, at the time of leaving, whether or not work-connected, is real, substantial and compelling and would cause a reasonable person genuinely desirous of retaining employment to leave work under the same circumstances. Although discharge for misconduct is not statutorily defined, factors used in determining the existence of misconduct include all of the following:

- A claimant owes a material duty to the employer under the contract of employment;

- There is a substantial breach of that duty;

- The breach is a willful or wanton disregard of that duty; and

- The breach disregards the employer's interests and injures or tends to injure the employer's interests.

Generally, an employee's inability to perform the duties of a job do not meet the definition of misconduct.

Suitable work means work in the employee's usual occupation, or for which he or she is reasonably fitted. Considerations for whether work is suitable include the:

- Degree of risk involved to the employee's health, safety and morals;

- Employee's physical fitness and prior training;

- Employee's experience and prior earnings;

- Length of unemployment and prospects for securing local work in the employee's customary occupation;

- Distance of the available work from the employee's residence; and

- Other factors that would influence a reasonably prudent person in the individual's circumstances.

UI benefits paid to an employee who left a job for a substantially better job and who later became eligible for UI (for example, because lost the job or had their hours reduced), are not chargeable to the account of the first employer. Employees who leave a job to protect themselves or their children from domestic violence abuse are deemed to have left *with* good cause. The employee is eligible for UI benefits if all other eligibility requirements are met. However, the UI benefits are not chargeable to the account of the employer.

For an extensive discussion of eligibility issues, see EDD's *Benefit Determination Guide* at **http://www.edd.ca.gov/uibdg/uibdgind.htm**. This *Guide* presents discussions about UI law, based on:

- State and federal laws;

- State and federal regulations;

- Case law from the United States Supreme Court, the California Supreme Court and lower federal and state courts; and

- Precedent Benefit Decisions issued by the California Unemployment Insurance Appeals Board.

It consists of eight volumes, each of which provides discussion on one broad issue of UI law. EDD personnel use the *Benefit Determination Guide* to make decisions about eligibility for UI benefits.

What You Should Do

Use the following sample checklists to determine whether to respond to a UI claim, how to respond properly and in the most effective manner. Specifically, the:

- *Responding to a Claim for Unemployment Insurance* checklist on the CD that comes with this product explains how to respond to a notice that a UI claim has been filed;

- *Appealing a UI Claim to an Administrative Law Judge* checklist on the CD that comes with this product describes how to appeal a claim to a judge if an employee has been awarded UI; and

- *Appealing a UI Claim to the UI Appeals Board* checklist on the CD that comes with this product shows you how to make a final appeal to the UI Board if the judge decides against you.

Keep the completed checklists in a file with the former employee's UI claim paperwork. The checklists can be maintained in the employee's personnel file.

The California Chamber's *2004 California Labor Law Digest* contains an entire chapter on the subject of UI. You can order it by calling (800) 331–8877, or visiting the

California Chamber store at ***http://www.calchamberstore.com***.You also may obtain more information on EDD's website at ***http://www.edd.ca.gov***.

What Forms and Checklists Do I Use to Manage Unemployment Compensation?

The following table describes forms and checklists associated with managing unemployment compensation.

 You can find these forms on the CD that comes with this product.

Table 22. Recommended Forms and Checklists

Form/ Checklist Name	What do I use it for?	When do I use it?	Who fills it out?	Where does it go?
Appealing a UI Claim to an Administrative Law Judge	To help you prepare an appeal to a judge for a UI claim you are protesting	During the appeal process	You do	Keep a copy in the employee's personnel file.
Appealing a UI Claim to the UI Appeals Board	To help guide you in presenting your final case to the UI Appeals Board	At the final stage of the appeal process after your appeal has been rejected by an ALJ	You do	Keep a copy in the employee's personnel file.
Responding to a Claim for Unemployment Insurance	Recommended for *all* types of separation	After the separation process	Employer uses checklists to fight UI claims	Keep the checklists in your personnel records.

Index

Helping California Business Do Business ®